"The often-repeated baptismal [...] the Son and of the Holy Spirit' [...] ever hear. They show us who God is, and they teach us who we are. That is why we need to grow in our understanding and experience of them. Scott Swain helps us to do that in this welcome contribution to Short Studies in Systematic Theology. The book lives up to its description: it is *short* (Swain gets straight to the point); it invites you to *study* (no superficiality here); and it is *systematic theology* (and Swain is exceptionally gifted in it). Plus, you will be able to understand Swain; and you can trust what he writes. What more could you ask for in such a compact treatment?"

Sinclair B. Ferguson, Chancellor's Professor of Systematic Theology, Reformed Theological Seminary; Teaching Fellow, Ligonier Ministries

"Only a very gifted teacher can select the most important things to say about the holy Trinity, especially for a wide audience. Lucid, rich with scriptural interpretation, and deeply informed by the Christian tradition, this is the first book I will recommend to anyone looking for clarity that yields a harvest of delight in the triune God."

Michael Horton, J. Gresham Machen Professor of Systematic Theology and Apologetics, Westminster Seminary California

"What a powerful instrument this little book is, meeting the need of our moment for clear and precise teaching on this most important subject. Would you rather read a book on the Trinity that invites you into the worship of God and gives profound insight into his ways or a book that is guaranteed to provide safe, reliable, and responsible instruction? There is no need to choose: this book does it all, and in admirably brief compass."

Fred Sanders, Professor of Theology, Torrey Honors Institute, Biola University; author, *The Deep Things of God*

"Swain here takes up the practice of the ancient church, teaching the company of the baptized the grammar of the name of the one God into whose life they enter by water: 'Father, Son, and Holy Spirit.' This is a wonderful primer to the grammar of 'Trinitarian discourse,' a grammar that is needed not simply to talk theological shop with the professionals but, more importantly, to read the Bible fluently, to name God correctly, to discern the true triune God from idols, and to praise the name of the one who invites us into the fellowship of the Father and the Son through the Spirit. This book edifies even as it educates."

> **Kevin J. Vanhoozer,** Research Professor of Systematic Theology, Trinity Evangelical Divinity School; author, *Is There a Meaning in This Text?*; *The Drama of Doctrine*; and *Biblical Authority after Babel*

"Through his attentive comprehension of Scripture and with prudence and ease, Scott Swain creates a profound and engaging portrayal of the triune God whom Christians worship. *The Trinity* will doubtless become the standard text for those requiring an accessible primer for this foundational doctrine. But the book's concise nature should not lull the expert, for Swain also offers persuasive verdicts defending classic orthodoxy against both contemporary and ancient challenges."

> **Malcolm B. Yarnell III,** Research Professor of Theology, Southwestern Baptist Theological Seminary; author, *Who Is the Holy Spirit?* and *God the Trinity*

"This book is easily the best introduction to the doctrine of the Trinity that I know of. Scott Swain shows not just *that* the Bible teaches the Trinity but *how* it does so. With lucid brevity he introduces crucial, classical distinctions that help us discern the Bible's Trinitarian grammar. Reading this book will help you to proclaim and praise the triune God more fluently. I plan to give away many copies to members of my church."

> **Bobby Jamieson,** Associate Pastor, Capitol Hill Baptist Church, Washington, DC; author, *Jesus' Death and Heavenly Offering in Hebrews*

The Trinity

SHORT STUDIES IN SYSTEMATIC THEOLOGY

Edited by Graham A. Cole and Oren R. Martin

The Trinity

An Introduction

Scott R. Swain

WHEATON, ILLINOIS

The Trinity: An Introduction

Copyright © 2020 by Scott R. Swain

Published by Crossway
        1300 Crescent Street
        Wheaton, Illinois 60187

Cover design: Jordan Singer

Cover image: From the New York Public Library, catalog ID (B-number): b14500417

First printing 2020

Printed in the United States of America

Trade paperback ISBN: 978-1-4335-6121-4
ePub ISBN: 978-1-4335-6124-5
PDF ISBN: 978-1-4335-6122-1
Mobipocket ISBN: 978-1-4335-6123-8

Library of Congress Cataloging-in-Publication Data

Names: Swain, Scott R., author. | Cole, Graham A. (Graham Arthur), 1949 editor. | Martin, Oren R., editor.

Title: The Trinity : an introduction / Scott R. Swain.

Description: Wheaton, Illinois : Crossway, 2020. | Series: Short studies in systematic theology | Includes bibliographical references and index.

Identifiers: LCCN 2020014773 (print) | LCCN 2020014774 (ebook) | ISBN 9781433561214 (trade paperback) | ISBN 9781433561221 (pdf) | ISBN 9781433561238 (mobipocket) | ISBN 9781433561245 (epub)

Subjects: LCSH: Trinity.

Classification: LCC BT111.3 .S945 2020 (print) | LCC BT111.3 (ebook) | DDC 231/.044—dc23

LC record available at https://lccn.loc.gov/2020014773

LC ebook record available at https://lccn.loc.gov/2020014774

Crossway is a publishing ministry of Good News Publishers.

VP		31	30	29	28	27	26	25	24	23	22	21
15	14	13	12	11	10	9	8	7	6	5	4	3

To four friends
valiant for the truth and honor
of the blessed Trinity

Aimee Byrd
Liam Goligher
Todd Pruitt
Carl Trueman

Contents

Series Preface

The ancient Greek thinker Heraclitus reputedly said that the thinker has to listen to the essence of things. A series of theological studies dealing with the traditional topics that make up systematic theology needs to do just that. Accordingly, in these studies, theologians address the essence of a doctrine. This series thus aims to present short studies in theology that are attuned to both the Christian tradition and contemporary theology in order to equip the church to faithfully understand, love, teach, and apply what God has revealed in Scripture about a variety of topics. What may be lost in comprehensiveness can be gained through what John Calvin, in the dedicatory epistle of his commentary on Romans, called "lucid brevity."

Of course, a thorough study of any doctrine will be longer rather than shorter, as there are two millennia of confession, discussion, and debate with which to interact. As a result, a short study needs to be more selective but deftly so. Thankfully, the contributors to this series have the ability to be brief yet accurate. The key aim is that the simpler is not to morph into the simplistic. The test is whether the topic of a short study, when further studied in depth, requires some unlearning to take place. The simple can be amplified. The simplistic needs to be corrected. As editors, we believe that the volumes in this series pass that test.

While the specific focus varies, each volume (1) introduces the doctrine, (2) sets it in context, (3) develops it from Scripture, (4) draws the various threads together, and (5) brings it to bear on the Christian life. It is our prayer, then, that this series will assist the church to delight in her triune God by thinking his thoughts—which he has graciously revealed in his written word, which testifies to his living Word, Jesus Christ—after him in the powerful working of his Spirit.

Graham A. Cole and Oren R. Martin

Acknowledgments

Under God's good providence, the present work has a deep cause and a proximate one. The deep cause is the long-standing encouragement of my wife, Leigh, that I write something on the Trinity for a popular audience. Though her suggested title, *You, Me, and the Trinity*, did not survive the publisher's scrutiny, this book is in large measure a response to her encouragement.

The proximate cause for the book is the Trinitarian controversy of 2016. That controversy revealed severe cracks in the foundation of evangelical Trinitarian theology. It also revealed the need for significant re-catechizing of the evangelical mind. I hope to make a small contribution to such re-catechizing in this study.

In addition to these two causes, thanks are due to many others who contributed to making this book possible. Chancellor Ligon Duncan and the Board of Trustees of Reformed Theological Seminary (especially Chairman Richard Ridgway and Admiral Scott Redd) have continued to encourage my pursuit of scholarship amid administrative and teaching responsibilities. Keith Whitfield, vice president for academic administration at Southeastern Baptist Theological Seminary in Wake Forest, North Carolina, generously provided a hospitable setting for research and writing on the beautiful campus of Southeastern in the summers of 2018 and 2019. Christina Mansfield provided research and administrative assistance with characteristic excellence and good cheer. My colleague Leigh Swanson read the entire manuscript and offered helpful recommendations for its improvement.

Justin Taylor and the good folks at Crossway have been a pleasure to work with on this project. I am also grateful to Graham Cole and Oren Martin for the invitation to contribute to their series and for their wise editorial oversight and advice.

Over the summer of 2016 I had hundreds of exchanges about the Trinity with four friends in particular: two pastors (Liam Goligher and Todd Pruitt), a lay theologian (Aimee Byrd), and a professor of church history (Carl Trueman). In gratitude for their courageous defense of orthodox Christian teaching on the Trinity in various settings and their recommendation that I contribute something to the discussion as well, I dedicate this book to them.

Introduction

Praising the Triune God

Christians praise one God in three persons, the blessed Trinity. We do so by proclaiming God's triune name in baptism (Matt. 28:19), by invoking his name in benedictions (2 Cor. 13:14), by binding ourselves to his name when confessing our faith (1 Cor. 8:6; 12:3), and by hymning his name in our songs, joining the chorus of heavenly beings with all the saints in heaven and earth (Rev. 4–5).

Christians praise God the Trinity because he is supremely worthy of our praise. The blessed Trinity is supreme in being, beauty, and beatitude.

> The LORD is a great God,
>   and a great King above all gods. (Ps. 95:3)

His "glory" is "above the heavens" (Ps. 8:1). He is "the blessed and only Sovereign, the King of kings and Lord of lords" (1 Tim. 6:15). Though the triune God is worthy of all the praise he receives (Rev. 4:11; 5:9–10, 12), our praise falls far short of his majestic greatness. He is God beyond all praising (Neh. 9:5), beyond all human comprehending. "His greatness is unsearchable" (Ps. 145:3).

Christians praise the triune God not only in response to the greatness of his being, beauty, and beatitude. We also praise him in response to the wonder of his works of creation, redemption, and consummation. The thrice-holy God is worthy "to receive glory and honor and power" because he "created all things" (Rev. 4:11). The Lamb who sits on the throne is worthy

> to receive power and wealth and wisdom and might
> and honor and glory and blessing! (Rev. 5:12)

For he redeemed us by his blood and made us a kingdom of priests to our God (Rev. 5:9–10). The Spirit is worthy of our praise because he opens our eyes to behold the majesty of God's being and works (Rev. 4:2–3), because he enables us to receive every spiritual blessing by his indwelling presence (Eph. 1:3), because he opens our lips to declare God's praise (1 Cor. 12:3; Gal. 4:6), and because he assures us that God will one day consummate his kingdom, in which—in and with our Lord Jesus Christ—we will reign on the earth as a kingdom of priests (Eph. 1:13–14; Rev. 5:10).

In praising God's triune name, we do not praise him as mere spectators, stunned before the magnificence of his being and works. Christian praise of God the Trinity is self-involving. The God who *is* Father, Son, and Holy Spirit, the author and end of all things, wills to be *our* Father, through the Son, in the Spirit. The blessed Trinity who dwells in a high and holy place, who inhabits eternity, whose name is holy, wills also to dwell among us and to make us eternally blessed through union and communion with him, to the praise of his glorious grace (Lev. 26:12; Isa. 57:15; John 14:23; 2 Cor. 6:16, 18; Eph. 1:3–14).

The self-involving nature of Christian faith in the Trinity is exhibited, perhaps most clearly, in Christian baptism. There the name of the triune God is proclaimed in the word of the minister and put on us with the washing of water (Matt. 28:19; Eph. 5:26). In baptism the God who is Father, Son, and Spirit signifies and seals to us that he is our Father, through union with the Son, by the indwelling of the Spirit and that we are God's sons and daughters, fellow heirs with Christ of an eternal kingdom (Rom. 8:17; Gal. 3:26; 4:6–7). Thereafter, the entire Christian life is about learning to "put on" the reality signified and sealed to us through baptism in God's triune name (Gal. 3:27), about receiving all that goes with having the triune God as our God, and about growing up into his praise within the communion of saints.[1]

A Short Study in Systematic Theology

In keeping with the aims of the larger series of which the present study is a part, this book is intended to be a "short study in systematic theology." Systematic theology, as a field of discourse, takes God and all things in relation to God as its object and Holy Scripture as its supreme source and norm. In doing so, systematic theology seeks to promote fluency, formation, and fellowship with the triune God among its major ends. A word about how each of these elements of systematic theology relates to the present topic is in order.

Systematic theology takes God and all things in relation to God as its object. Systematic theology focuses on God: his being, attributes, persons, and decrees; as well as the works of God: creation, providence, redemption, sanctification, and consummation. In each instance, God is the organizing principle of systematic theology. When considering any doctrine, systematic theology asks, how does this doctrine relate to God as its author and end (Rom. 11:36)? Thus, for example,

---

1. Basil of Caesarea, *On the Holy Spirit*, trans. Stephen Hildebrand (Yonkers, NY: St Vladimir's Seminary Press, 2011), 10.26.

systematic theology does not consider human beings in general terms. It considers human beings as creatures made in the image of God, as rebels who have sinned against God, thereby bringing misery upon themselves, and as objects of God's redeeming, sanctifying, and consummating work. The specific focus of the present study is the principal subject matter of systematic theology: the blessed Trinity in his being and works.

Systematic theology takes Holy Scripture as its supreme source and norm. God reveals himself in a multitude of ways: through creation and conscience, through miracles and theophanies, and supremely through his Son, our Lord Jesus Christ (Rom. 1:18–32; Heb. 1:1–4). Holy Scripture is God's Spirit-inspired testimony to Jesus Christ. As such, Holy Scripture is the supreme source and norm for our knowledge of the triune God in his being and works (2 Tim. 3:15–17). In this book, our main focus is on the scriptural patterns of naming the triune God and the way those patterns have been received and confessed by the church in response to the triune God's self-revelation in Holy Scripture.

Among its major ends, systematic theology seeks to promote fluency, formation, and fellowship. Because it focuses on God and all things in relation to God as these realities are revealed in Holy Scripture, systematic theology aims at making us more fluent readers of Holy Scripture. Because the God who reveals himself in Holy Scripture also writes its message on our hearts by the Holy Spirit, systematic theology seeks to serve the Spirit's work of forming in us the image of Jesus Christ. In this regard, systematic theology seeks to shape our judgment, our affections, and our actions. Finally, systematic theology seeks to promote fellowship with the object of theology, God himself. God is the sovereign good that systematic theology pursues, and fellowship with God (and with one another in God) is the supreme means of engaging with God the sovereign good.

How does this volume relate to these various ends? It seeks to cultivate greater fluency in following the basic "grammar" of Scripture's Trinitarian discourse.[2] In so doing, the present study seeks to form Christian judgment—specifically, the capacity for distinguishing the true and living God from idols. This study also aims to shape our capacities for receiving and responding to the blessed Trinity as he presents himself to us in his word: directing our faith to receive the triune God as our God, to hold fast to the triune God in love, and to call upon the triune God in prayer, proclamation, and praise. Finally, the present study seeks to promote fellowship with the triune God, the sovereign good of systematic theology. Ultimately our fluency as readers of Holy Scripture and our formation in Christian virtue are ordered to this supreme end, the triune God himself, who gives himself to us as our supreme good in the grace of our Lord Jesus Christ, the love of God the Father, and the fellowship of the Holy Spirit (2 Cor. 13:14).

As a species of catechetical theology, this "short study" in systematic theology intends to offer a brief introduction to Christian teaching on the holy Trinity, with a focus on scriptural patterns of divine naming. The book's limitations in space and focus mean that it will not give extensive attention to the doctrine's historical development, polemical uses, or more

---

2. In order to grasp any distinct field of discourse, we must grasp not only the meaning of various terms used within that field (i.e., its "lexicon") but also the relationships that obtain between various terms used within that field (i.e., its "syntax"). Taken together, the lexicon and syntax that distinguish a particular field of discourse constitute its basic "grammar" (Paul J. Griffiths, *The Practice of Catholic Theology: A Modest Proposal* [Washington, DC: Catholic University of America Press, 2016], 97–105). If Scripture provides the primary discourse of Trinitarian doctrine, theology is that discipline concerned with understanding and communicating Scripture's basic grammar so that Christians may become fluent, well-formed readers and speakers of scriptural teaching.

sophisticated dogmatic elaborations. Nevertheless, I hope that by introducing the basic grammar of scriptural Trinitarianism, this book may encourage more advanced study of these other topics as well.[3]

This work is designed to serve beginning students of theology, whether enrolled in a formal program of theological study or not, pastors seeking to review the main contours of Trinitarian teaching, and interested laypersons. In each case, it is written to help Christians enter more fully into the praise of the triune name into which we are baptized. How shall we proceed?

An Overview of Chapters

Christians praise the triune God because that is how God presents himself to us in Holy Scripture: as one God in three persons, the Father, the Son, and the Holy Spirit. By his word, God reveals his triune name in Holy Scripture. By his Spirit, God takes his triune name, as revealed in Holy Scripture, and writes it on our hearts, training us to call upon his name in prayer, proclamation, and praise. For this reason, the God-breathed Scriptures are the primary discourse of Trinitarian theology. Thus, we commence our study with a survey of scriptural teaching on the Trinity.

Taking the triune name in which we were baptized as our starting point (Matt. 28:19), chapter 1 considers various patterns of biblical discourse that reflect the grammar of God's triune name. Chapter 2 then moves to consider representative biblical texts that can assist us in gaining greater fluency in the praise of God's triune name, concluding with a summary of biblical teaching on the Trinity.

---

3. For further discussion of the historical development of the doctrine of the Trinity, see Stephen R. Holmes, *The Quest for the Trinity: The Doctrine of God in Scripture, History, and Modernity* (Downers Grove, IL: IVP Academic, 2012); and Carl L. Beckwith, *The Holy Trinity* (Ft. Wayne, IN: The Luther Academy, 2016).

Following our survey of the Bible's primary Trinitarian discourse, we turn to a more thematic treatment of the doctrine in chapters 3–8. Because baptism identifies God in himself (Matt. 28:19), we contemplate, first, the one God in his internal relations as Father, Son, and Spirit (chaps. 3–6). Because baptism also identifies God in relation to us (Gal. 3:26–27), we contemplate, second, the one God in his external relations whereby, through his external works, he becomes our Father, through the Son, by the Spirit, to the praise of his glory (chaps. 7–8).

Christian teaching on the Trinity is teaching about the one God. Chapter 3 thus considers the doctrine of divine simplicity, an essential feature of orthodox Trinitarian theology. Chapters 4–6 then look at the three persons that constitute the life of the one God. Chapter 4 considers the person of the Father, chapter 5 the person of the Son, and chapter 6 the person of the Holy Spirit. Over the course of these chapters, I address topics such as the nature of analogical language, the nature of divine persons, and important matters of controversy in Trinitarian theology (e.g., the question of eternal relations of authority and submission between the Father and the Son).

Chapters 7–8 then consider the triune God in his external works. Chapter 7 looks at the shape of God's triune work, giving attention to the "appropriation" of specific works to specific persons of the Trinity, as well as to the "missions" of the Son and the Spirit.

Chapter 8 looks at the end of God's triune work (i.e., God himself), along with the beneficiaries of God's triune work (i.e., his beloved children) and the means whereby God communicates himself to his beloved children through the ministry of word and sacrament, which are received by faith, hope, and love. In attending to the latter topics, chapter 8 sketches in brief outline a Trinitarian theology of ministry and the Christian life.

Conclusion

No topic of study is more rewarding, or more challenging, than the doctrine of the Trinity. Nor is any topic of study fraught with greater possibility of error.[4] Nevertheless, we may enter our study with confidence because the triune God has revealed himself in his word. It is God's good pleasure that we would know him, that we would receive him, and that our souls would find rest in him (Matt. 11:25–30).

Moreover, in spite of the many limitations of our study— we know only in part, not yet face-to-face (1 Cor. 13:12); we are both finite and fallen—God has promised sure help for our study through Jesus Christ our Redeemer, the Lion and the Lamb (Rev. 4–5). In union with Jesus Christ, by the Spirit, we have access to the Father (Eph. 2:18). And so we may confidently pray,

> Let my soul live and praise you,
>   and let your rules help me. (Ps. 119:175)

Learning to praise the blessed Trinity holds broad implications for many fields of discourse, from metaphysics to epistemology, from ethics to aesthetics. That said, learning to praise the Trinity does not derive its importance or usefulness from its ability to serve other enterprises. Learning to know the triune God, to receive the triune God, to rejoice in the triune God—and learning to help others do the same—is an end in itself, because the triune God is the ultimate end of all things (Rom. 11:36).

---

4. Augustine, *The Trinity*, trans. Edmund Hill (Brooklyn, NY: New City, 1991), 1.5.

Here is the treasure hidden in a field and the pearl of great price: knowing, receiving, loving, and praising the Father, through the Son, in the fellowship of the Spirit (Matt. 13:44–46; John 17:3). To him be glory forever.

1

The Bible and the Trinity

The Basic Grammar

Christians praise the triune God because that is how God presents himself to us in Holy Scripture: as one God in three persons, the Father, the Son, and the Holy Spirit. The Bible is the primary discourse of Trinitarian theology. Fluently, almost effortlessly, the prophets and apostles narrate, bless, pray, and sing the name of the triune God. In its own mysterious way, the Old Testament speaks of the Trinity, portraying God as a sovereign speech agent who created all things by his Word and Spirit (Gen. 1:1–3; Ps. 33:6, 9), inviting us to overhear conversations between the Lord and his anointed Son (Pss. 2; 110), and prompting us to wonder about the threefold repetition of YHWH's name in the Aaronic Benediction (Num. 6:22–27) and about the true identity of Wisdom in Proverbs 8.

The veiled riddles of Old Testament Trinitarian revelation are resolved in the New Testament's announcement of the incarnation of the Son and the outpouring of the Spirit. Often-times taking up the express language of the Old Testament, the New Testament draws more definitive lines in portraits only sketched in Old Testament texts (compare Gen. 1:1–3 with John 1:1–3), clarifies the identity of speakers in otherwise ambiguous Old Testament conversations (compare Ps. 2 with Heb. 1, and Ps. 110 with Mark 12:35–37), and recognizes Wisdom as more than a literary personification, identifying him as God's beloved Son, the image of the invisible God, the firstborn of all creation (Col. 1:13–20; Heb. 1:3). The primary discourse of New Testament Trinitarianism includes the heavenly pronouncements overheard at Jesus's baptism and at the Mount of Transfiguration (Matt. 3:17; 17:5), the praise and petitions Jesus offers his Father (Matt. 11:25–27; John 17), and the various triadic patterns that occur in baptismal formulas (Matt. 28:19), blessings (Eph. 1:3–14), and benedictions (2 Cor. 13:14).

The climax of God's work of redemption brings with it the climax of God's triune self-revelation.

> But when the fullness of time had come, God sent forth his Son, born of a woman, born under the law, to redeem those who were under the law, so that we might receive adoption as sons. And because you are sons, God has sent the Spirit of his Son into our hearts, crying, "Abba! Father!" So you are no longer a slave, but a son, and if a son, then an heir through God. (Gal. 4:4–7)

The God who is Father, Son, and Spirit has reached out through the Son and by the Spirit to embrace us as sons and daughters to the end that we may call God our Father in the Spirit of the Son.

What we find in later Trinitarian creeds, confessions, and doctrinal summaries are not improvements upon a latent or undeveloped biblical Trinitarianism but, rather, the church's attempt to fathom the depth of the riches of biblical Trinitarianism for the sake of various liturgical, pedagogical, and polemical ends. Some of the church's creeds, confessions, and doctrinal summaries represent such faithful expressions of scriptural teaching and enjoy such wide-ranging ecclesiastical consensus that we dare not transgress the lines they have drawn. Rather, taking them on our own lips, we gladly join the church's chorus of Trinitarian praise.

Even then, scriptural Trinitarianism retains its status as primary Trinitarian discourse, not just in the sense that the Bible's Trinitarian discourse is the source and norm of Trinitarian doctrine, but also in the sense that the Bible's Trinitarian discourse is Trinitarian theology's normative "pattern" (2 Tim. 1:13) and generative "standard" (Rom. 6:17) for fluent, well-formed Trinitarian praise: its grammar, its lexicon, and its syntax. Everything else is commentary.

If this is so, then the primary task of Trinitarian theology is to gain fluency in the Bible's primary Trinitarian discourse. We must learn to read it well. We must learn to grasp its terms, to follow its patterns, to make the identifications it makes, to mark the distinctions it marks. We must master its grammar. And we must learn to put that grammar to use in our own well-formed speech acts of prayer, proclamation, and praise of God's triune name. The purpose of the present chapter and the next is to assist us in this task.

As we saw in the introduction, we were baptized into God's triune name so that we might learn to praise God's triune name. The triune name into which we were baptized, "the name of the Father and of the Son and of the Holy Spirit" (Matt. 28:19), encapsulates the basic grammar, the ABCs, of scriptural Trinitarianism. It thus provides a helpful starting point for familiarizing ourselves with the basic patterns of the Bible's Trinitarian discourse. Following a discussion of the basic grammar of scriptural Trinitarianism in this chapter, the next chapter will consider three types of scriptural texts that give us a fuller sense of the Bible's Trinitarian discourse.

Baptized into the Name of the Triune God

By encapsulating the basic grammar of the Bible's Trinitarian discourse, Matthew 28:19 provides a helpful rubric for tracing various patterns of biblical Trinitarian discourse and for gaining facility in Trinitarian praise.

"The Name . . ."

The first thing to observe in Matthew's baptismal formula is that "the name" into which we are baptized is singular, not plural. The faith into which we are baptized is faith in the one God. "For us there is one God," "one Lord" (1 Cor. 8:6), "one Spirit" (Eph. 4:4).

Note, then, a first pattern: *the Bible's Trinitarian discourse consistently affirms the existence of the one God.*

The Bible acknowledges the existence of many religions that worship many gods, and it constantly warns us of the snare that these gods pose to God's people. However, the Bible also insists that these gods are gods in name only (1 Cor. 8:5). In truth, they are "no gods," "the work of men's hands" (Isa. 37:19; Jer. 2:11, 28).[1] The Lord alone is *"the* God" (Deut. 4:35, my trans.). He alone is

> a great God,
> and a great King above all gods. (Ps. 95:3)

---

1. When the existence of other gods is acknowledged, they are identified as "demons" (Deut. 32:17; Ps. 106:37–38; 1 Cor. 10:20–21; Rev. 9:20; see also 2 Cor. 4:4).

He alone is the author and end of all things (Gen. 1:1; Isa. 41:4; 44:6, 24; John 1:1–3; Rom. 11:33–36; 1 Cor. 8:6; Col. 1:15–20), "the Alpha and the Omega, the first and the last, the beginning and the end" (Rev. 22:13). What Moses teaches, Jesus confirms: the Lord is one and there is no other besides him (Deut. 4:35, 39; 6:4; Mark 12:29, 32).

One way Paul, the apostle to the Gentiles, signals God's uniqueness over against the gods is by appealing to the distinction, common in antiquity, between those that are "called" gods for honorific reasons (e.g., Caesar) and those that are gods "by nature," the latter possessing perfections, such as immortality, which are exclusive to the divine nature (Rom. 1:23; 1 Cor. 8:5; Gal. 4:8–9). Unlike much of antiquity, however, Paul insists that there is only one God who fits the bill in this regard. *All* other gods are "those that by nature are not gods" (Gal. 4:8). The significance is clear: the one God of Christian confession is not a member of a larger class of gods. He alone is God because he alone is God by nature, "the blessed and only Sovereign, the King of kings and Lord of lords, who alone has immortality, who dwells in unapproachable light" (1 Tim. 6:15–16).

The Bible's primary way of signaling God's uniqueness is by means of God's proper name, YHWH, often referred to as the "tetragrammaton" because it is composed of four Hebrew letters. As we have seen, the Bible frequently uses the title "god" to refer both to the one God and to those that are not actually gods. Furthermore, as I will discuss more fully in later chapters, the Bible uses an almost endless variety of creaturely terms to refer to the one God. God is called "Father," "King," "Maker," "refuge," and so forth. However, the Bible reserves the proper name YHWH for God alone. It is the one God's "holy name" (Ps. 145:21), the glory he will not share with another (Isa. 48:11).

Because of its uniqueness, YHWH is a name that only God can interpret to us. Thankfully, God has done just that. The book of Exodus is, in many respects, YHWH's self-interpretation writ large. According to Exodus, the name YHWH signifies God's self-existence. He is the consuming fire that requires no fuel in order to burn (Ex. 3:2–3). The name YHWH signifies God's self-identity or simplicity (Ex. 3:14). God is identical with his existence (John 5:26) and his attributes (1 John 1:5); from age to age, he is the selfsame, eternal and unchanging (Ps. 102:27). The name YHWH also signifies God's self-determination to accomplish his sovereign purpose, unrivaled in the face of his enemies (Ex. 9:16), and to demonstrate his unbounded sovereign goodness in maintaining steadfast love and faithfulness toward unworthy sinners (Ex. 33:19; 34:6–7). This is the name of the Lord according to the Lord. "Holy is his name" (Luke 1:49).

Greek translations of the Old Testament often render God's proper name, YHWH, by the Greek term *kyrios* or "lord," a convention that the New Testament follows as well, along with many English translations. So, for example, where the Hebrew Bible of Joel 2:32 commends calling on the name of YHWH, the Greek translation of this passage, as well as the New Testament passages that quote it, commend calling on "the name of the Lord" (Acts 2:21; Rom. 10:13).

"The Name of . . ."

This brings us back to Matthew 28:19. "The name" (singular!) in Matthew's baptismal formula is likely an "oblique reference" to God's proper name, YHWH.[2] Much like the title "Lord," it serves as a "surrogate" for the tetragrammaton.[3] This leads

---

2. R. Kendall Soulen, *The Divine Name(s) and the Holy Trinity*, vol. 1, *Distinguishing the Voices* (Louisville: Westminster John Knox, 2011), 176.

3. Soulen, *The Divine Name(s)*, 12.

us, in turn, to a second observation regarding Matthew's baptismal formula. If "the name" is a reference to God's proper name, YHWH, then, according to Matthew, the holy name of the Lord, the name that signifies—above all other names—the uniqueness of the one God, belongs to these three: the Father, the Son, and the Holy Spirit. These three are the one God.

Note, then, a second pattern: *the Bible's Trinitarian discourse consistently identifies the Father, the Son, and the Holy Spirit with the one God.*

As we observed above, though the Bible recognizes the worship of many gods, occasionally acknowledging their (demonic!) existence, the Bible clearly affirms the existence of only one true God, the author and end of all things. The Bible, moreover, distinguishes the one God not only from all other would-be gods but also from all creatures by his unique name, YHWH or "the Lord," and by his unique perfections. The Lord God does not share his glory with another (Isa. 48:11). According to the entire witness of Holy Scripture, the Father, the Son, and the Holy Spirit are not three gods. Nor are they some confederation of the one God with lesser gods. These three are the one God.

First Corinthians 8:6 is representative of a broad pattern of biblical teaching in this regard: "For us there is one God, the Father, from whom are all things and for whom we exist, and one Lord, Jesus Christ, through whom are all things and through whom we exist." This text identifies the Father and Jesus Christ with the one God, appropriating the language of Deuteronomy 6:4. And it places both the Father and Jesus Christ on the divine side of the distinction between the one God and "all things." We see similar patterns of identification in other biblical texts with respect to the Holy Spirit. The Spirit is identified with the one Lord God (Acts 5:3–4; 2 Cor. 3:17–18; Eph. 4:4), the

Maker of all things (Gen. 1:2; Ps. 33:6), to whom all praise and devotion are due (Matt. 12:31; 28:19).

"The Name of the Father and of the Son and of the Holy Spirit"

The third thing to observe in Matthew's baptismal formula is that, while the three are identified with the one God, they are nevertheless distinguished from each other by their personal names "the Father," "the Son," and "the Holy Spirit." As should be clear by now, the distinction between the three persons[4] does not amount to a distinction between three Gods: there is *one* Spirit, *one* Lord, and *one* God the Father of all (Eph. 4:4–6). Nevertheless, the distinction between the three persons is real. The three are truly identical with the one God, and they are truly distinct from each other. What, then, is the nature of the distinction between the three? The answer lies in the personal names themselves—"Father," "Son," and "Spirit"—and in the way these names are illustrated and coordinated in the Bible's Trinitarian discourse.

Note, then, a third pattern: *the Bible's Trinitarian discourse consistently distinguishes the Father, the Son, and the Holy Spirit by their mutual relations, which are "relations of origin."*

According to the Bible's Trinitarian discourse, the personal names "Father," "Son," and "Spirit" name *mutual relations—* that is, relations between the persons. The Father is the "Father of our Lord Jesus Christ" (Eph. 1:3; 1 Pet. 1:3). The Son is the Father's "beloved Son" (Matt. 3:17; Rom. 8:32; Gal. 4:4). The Holy Spirit is "the Spirit of God" (Matt. 3:16; 1 Cor. 2:11) and "the Spirt of Christ," "the Spirit of his Son" (Rom. 8:9; Gal. 4:6). What distinguishes the persons of the Trinity from each

---

4. I will discuss the origin of the term "person" in Trinitarian theology below. I will discuss the meaning of the concept in later chapters.

other are their relations to each other, not their relations to us. In fact, as we will see more fully in later chapters, the relations that the three persons hold toward us—for example, Creator, Redeemer, Lord—are something that the three persons hold in common as the one God, not something that distinguishes them from each other.

These relations, while mutual, are also *asymmetrical*. The Father eternally begets the Son (Ps. 2:7; John 1:18; 3:16; Heb. 1:5), not vice versa. The Father and the Son eternally breathe forth the Spirit (John 15:26; 20:22), not vice versa. In other words, the personal names of the Trinity distinguish the persons by means of "relations of origin." The Father personally originates from no one. The Son personally originates from the person of the Father. And the Spirit personally originates from the persons of the Father and the Son.

The Bible further illumines these relations of origin by employing various titles or illustrations to describe the persons, which are often drawn from the Old Testament and other Jewish writings.[5] The Son is identified as the "Word" of God (John 1:1; Rev. 19:13), the "image" of the invisible God (Col. 1:15), and the "radiance" of the Father's glory (Heb. 1:3). Each of these titles or illustrations reveals two things about the Son. On the one hand, these titles reveal that the Son is the one God in common with the Father. The Word is God (John 1:1). The image of the invisible God is the one by whom, in whom, and for whom creation exists (Col. 1:16–17). The radiance of God's glory is the exact imprint of the Father's substance (Heb. 1:3). On the other hand, these titles or illustrations also indicate what distinguishes the Father from the Son within the one God, namely, that the person of the Father is the eternal source of the

---

5. This and the following paragraph draw closely upon Scott R. Swain, "Divine Trinity," in *Christian Dogmatics: Reformed Theology for the Church Catholic*, ed. Michael Allen and Scott R. Swain (Grand Rapids, MI: Baker Academic, 2016).

person of the Son: the Son is the Word *of* God, the image *of* the invisible God, the radiance *of* the Father's glory. Relations of origin are relations of "from-ness."

In similar fashion, the Bible illustrates the Spirit's relation to the Father and the Son as a relation of origin. Particularly instructive are illustrations that associate the Holy Spirit with water. The Spirit is "poured" out by the Father (Rom. 5:5) and by the Son (Acts 2:33). He is the element with which Jesus baptizes his disciples (Mark 1:8; 1 Cor. 12:13). And he is the living water that flows from the throne of God and of the Lamb (Rev. 22:1). This imagery at once identifies the Holy Spirit with the one God as the divine source of spiritual life and as one who personally proceeds from the person of the Father and from the person of the Son.

Conclusion: Common Predication and Proper Predication

We will explore these patterns more fully in the chapters that follow. For now, it is important to take stock of what we have observed. As we noted above, gaining fluency in the Bible's Trinitarian discourse requires learning to make the right identifications and to mark the right distinctions. In surveying the Bible's Trinitarian discourse under the rubric of Matthew's baptismal formula, we observed patterns of divine naming that *identify* the three persons with the one God and patterns that *distinguish* the three persons from each other. In light of these two patterns, it will be useful to give each of them a label: *Common predications* are patterns of speech that refer to what the three persons of the Trinity hold in common with each other as the one God. They are "the Lord." They are the author and end of all creatures. And so forth. *Proper predications* are patterns of speech that refer to that which distinguishes the three persons of the Trinity from each other within the one God. This one is the Father of the Son. That one is the Son of the Father. And that one is the Spirit of the Father and the Son. And so forth.

Familiarity with these two patterns of divine naming, and the ability to identify them by their labels, will grant us greater fluency in reading the Bible's Trinitarian discourse moving forward and in understanding important discussions in the chapters ahead. Familiarity with these patterns will also grant us greater fluency as we seek to fulfill our baptismal vow in petitioning, proclaiming, and praising God's triune name, which is the point of Trinitarian theology.

2

The Bible and the Trinity

Three Types of Texts

Christians praise the triune God because that is how God presents himself to us in Holy Scripture: as one God in three persons, the Father, the Son, and the Holy Spirit. In the previous chapter we considered the basic grammar of the Bible's Trinitarian discourse as summarized in the baptismal mandate of Matthew 28:19. In the present chapter, we will consider three types of biblical texts that give us a fuller sense of the Bible's Trinitarian discourse. A brief summary of biblical teaching on the Trinity will round out the chapter.

Three Types of Biblical Texts That Speak about the Trinity

Having considered the ABCs of the Bible's Trinitarian discourse under the rubric of Matthew's baptismal formula, we turn now to three types of biblical texts that are especially important to biblical teaching on the Trinity. First, we will consider "inner-Trinitarian conversation texts," where we overhear the persons of the Trinity speaking to and of each other. Second, we will consider "cosmic framework texts," which frame the entire cosmos, as well as the entirety of God's work in the cosmos, in relation to the Trinity. Third, we will consider "redemptive mission texts," which display the sending or "mission" of the Son (and, sometimes, the sending of the Spirit) as the great divine acts whereby God fulfills his redemptive purpose, establishing his dwelling among us, for the praise of his name.

Inner-Trinitarian Conversation Texts

As we observed earlier, because of its uniqueness, the name YHWH is one that God himself must interpret to us if we are to appreciate and adore its significance. We come to know the meaning of God's holy name YHWH only by means of divine self-naming. This is also true when it comes to a knowledge of the persons of the Trinity: if we are to know the persons of the Trinity, the persons themselves must reveal themselves to us: "No one knows the Son except the Father, and no one knows the Father except the Son and anyone to whom the Son chooses to reveal him" (Matt. 11:27; see also John 1:18; 1 Cor. 2:10–11). The reason for this is not that "father," "son," and "spirit" are unique terms, never applied to would-be gods or creatures. It is that the persons of the Trinity belong to the "inside" of the one God's life. Knowledge of the persons of the Trinity is "insider knowledge," known to outsiders only when insiders make it known to them.[1]

Consider Paul's analogy in 1 Corinthians 2:11: "For who knows a person's thoughts except the spirit of that person,

---

1. Fred Sanders, *The Triune God*, New Studies in Dogmatics (Grand Rapids, MI: Zondervan Academic, 2016), 38.

which is in him?" Paul's analogy helps us appreciate one of the important differences between God's revelation through his works and God's self-revelation through his word. While creation reveals many things about the Creator, much as a work of art reveals many things about an artist, there are some things we can know about an artist only if he himself speaks to us, opening up to us the depths of his inner life. So it is with the Trinity. Because the persons of the Trinity are internal to God's life, not external works of God, we can know the persons of the Trinity, as well as their ultimate plan for creation (Eph. 3:9), only if they stoop down and open up the depths of their inner life to us. Only the persons of the Trinity know the persons of the Trinity. Therefore, only the persons of the Trinity can make known the persons of the Trinity. The revelation of the Trinity is a matter of divine *self*-revelation, divine *self*-presentation, divine *self*-naming.

Biblical texts where we overhear inner-Trinitarian conversations—conversations where the persons of the Trinity speak to or about each other—are among the Bible's primary modes of Trinitarian self-revelation. One example of an inner-Trinitarian conversation comes in Matthew's, Mark's, and Luke's accounts of Jesus's baptism. There we overhear the Father speaking of/to the Son, "This is my beloved Son, with whom I am well pleased" (Matt. 3:16–17; see also Mark 1:10–11; Luke 3:21–22). Viewed within the overarching structure of Matthew's Gospel, it seems Matthew wants to teach us that one of the reasons *we* baptize in "the name of the Father and of the Son and of the Holy Spirit" (Matt. 28:19) is that, at Jesus's baptism, *the Father* called Jesus his beloved Son and anointed him with his Holy Spirit (Matt. 3:16–17). Divine Trinitarian self-naming is the foundation of our baptismal naming of the triune God.

Another example of an inner-Trinitarian conversation comes in Matthew 11:25–27. There Jesus breaks out in praise, addressing the Father:

> I thank you, Father, Lord of heaven and earth, that you have hidden these things from the wise and understanding and revealed them to little children; yes, Father, for such was your gracious will. All things have been handed over to me by my Father, and no one knows the Son except the Father, and no one knows the Father except the Son and anyone to whom the Son chooses to reveal him.

Several features of this passage are worth noting. First, Jesus identifies the "Lord of heaven and earth" as his "Father," and he identifies himself as the Father's "Son." To recall our earlier labels, this is an example of "proper predication"—that is, predication that distinguishes one person of the Trinity from another person of the Trinity. Second, Jesus claims that the authority that belongs to his Father as Lord of heaven and earth also belongs to him because the Father has granted it to him. Again, to recall our earlier label, this is an example of "common predication"—that is, predication that identifies what the persons of the Trinity hold in common as the one God. Third, as we observed above, Matthew 11:25–27 is a classic example of a text indicating that the knowledge of the Trinity is a matter of "insider knowledge." The only reason *we* come to know the persons of the Trinity is that *they* name themselves in our hearing.[2] Fourth, as in Matthew's account of Jesus's baptism, Matthew 11:25–27 anticipates the baptismal formula of Matthew

---

2. Luke's account of the same incident makes two related points. On the one hand, Jesus's doxology is a fully *Trinitarian* event because Jesus rejoices "in the Holy Spirit" in offering his praise to the Father (Luke 10:21). On the other hand, this incident of Trinitarian self-naming is taken as representative of the apostles' unique access to the revelation of God's triune name and purpose and therefore serves as a foundation for the apostles' authority to proclaim God's triune name and purpose (Luke 10:23–24).

28:19 by identifying Jesus as the Son who, with the Father and from the Father, has "all authority" (Matt. 28:18) to demand the discipleship of "all nations" through baptism and instruction (Matt. 28:19) and to guarantee the success of the Great Commission by his divine presence (Matt. 28:20).[3]

One final example of an inner-Trinitarian conversation comes in Hebrews 1:5: "For to which of the angels did God ever say: 'You are my Son, today I have begotten you'?"[4] Hebrews 1:5 offers an interpretation of Psalm 2:7 that seeks to demonstrate the superiority of the Son, as God's divine ambassador, over angels, God's heavenly but creaturely ambassadors. In so doing, the author of Hebrews engages in an interpretive technique, common in the ancient world, known as "prosopological exegesis." *Prosōpon* is a Greek term for "person." In prosopological exegesis, an interpreter clarifies the identities of persons speaking or spoken to in texts where their identities are otherwise ambiguous. Thus, in the case of Psalm 2:7, while the identity of the speaker is clearly YHWH ("The LORD [YHWH] said to me"—Ps. 2:7), the identity of the person to whom he speaks is not. Is the Lord addressing David, one of David's sons, someone else, or perhaps all of the above? According to the author of Hebrews, the answer is clear: in Psalm 2:7, the Lord is addressing the "person" of his divine Son.

How do we know this? Recall the context of Hebrews 1:5. The author is seeking to establish the superiority of Jesus over the angels. If the Lord were merely addressing one of David's human sons in Psalm 2:7, then the citation would not work. Why not? Because the author explicitly states in Hebrews 2:7 (citing Ps. 8) that human beings are "lower than the angels."

---

3. Compare with Matt. 1:23, where the Son is called "Immanuel" or "God with us."

4. For more extensive analysis of this text, see Madison Pierce, "Hebrews 1 and the Son Begotten 'Today,'" in *Retrieving Eternal Generation*, ed. Fred Sanders and Scott R. Swain (Grand Rapids, MI: Zondervan Academic, 2017).

Jesus is superior to angels, the author of Hebrews insists, because he is YHWH's divine Son.

Several other features of Hebrews 1:5 are worth observing. First, Hebrews 1:5 says something about the nature of the "relation of origin" that constitutes the Son's relation to the Father. Hebrews 1:5 teaches that the Son is "begotten" of the Father, and it teaches that the "timing" of the Son's begetting occurs in the eternal, unchanging "today" of God's triune life.[5] The Son is thus superior to angels because he is eternally begotten, not made (compare Heb. 1:7, which refers to the created nature of angels).

Second, if this reading is correct, then it says something not only about the Son's relation to the Father but also about the Son's relation to creation. The progression of Hebrews 1:2–4

---

5. That the "today" of Heb. 1:5 refers to God's eternity seems clear for three reasons: (1) Heb. 1:2–4 ascribes an array of attributes and activities to the Son to demonstrate his superiority over the angels: he was appointed the heir of all things; he created the world; he is the radiance of God's glory and the exact imprint of his substance; he upholds the world by the word of his power; he made purification for sins; he sat down at the right hand of the Father; he has inherited a more excellent name than the angels. A natural reading of this array of attributes and activities suggests that the Son was appointed the heir of all things *before* he created all things. Why is this relevant? Because the claim of Heb. 1:2 that God appointed the Son to be the heir of all things is likely an allusion to Ps. 2:8 ("Ask of me, and I will make the nations your heritage, / and the ends of the earth your possession"), the same psalm that speaks of the "timing" of the Son's begetting. The author of Hebrews thus seems to view both the Son's begetting and the Son's being appointed heir of all things as having occurred before creation in God's eternal life. (2) The eternity of the Son is a major theme in Heb. 1. In Heb. 1:8–9, the author cites Ps. 45:6–7 to prove that the Son's kingdom will endure throughout eternity. In Heb. 1:10–11, the author cites Ps. 102:25–27 to prove that the Son is YHWH, the eternal, unchanging Creator of all temporal, changeable creatures. Reading Heb. 1:5 as referring to the Son's eternal begetting is thus entirely in keeping with the rest of Heb. 1. (3) The eternity of the Son is a major theme throughout the letter to the Hebrews. In Heb. 7:3, the author draws a comparison between Jesus, the eternal Son of God, and Melchizedek, stating that the latter "is without father or mother or genealogy, having neither beginning of days nor end of life, but resembling the Son of God he continues a priest forever." Similarly, in Heb. 13:8, the author says, "Jesus Christ is the same yesterday and today and forever." This verse is significant because the author uses two terms to describe the unchanging eternity of the Son ("today" and "the same") that he has already used in Heb. 1:5 ("today") and 1:12 ("the same"). Given the author's other uses of the term "today" to describe the unchanging and abiding eternity of God's Word (Heb. 3:7, 13, 15; 4:7), the implication seems clear: the "today" of the Father's begetting of the Son is an "eternal" begetting.

moves from the eternal appointment of the Son as the heir of all things to his creation of all things, to his providential preservation of all things, to his atoning work, to his exaltation at the Father's right hand, culminating in his public reception of a name more excellent than the angels. According to Hebrews, creation is *from* the Father's eternally begotten Son. Creation is redeemed *by* the Father's eternally begotten Son. And creation exists *for* the Father's eternally begotten Son, to be his inheritance. The *person* of the Son is the *purpose* of creation. He is why creation exists, and he is what creation is for. Within the argument of Hebrews 1, the relationship between the Son and creation provides yet another reason for the Son's superiority to angels, and a reason for the summons issued in Hebrews 1:6:

> When he brings the firstborn into the world, he says,
>
> "Let all God's angels worship him."

All things are by and for God's eternally begotten Son; to him be glory forever.

Third, and more broadly, the interpretation of inner-Trinitarian conversations in Old Testament texts by New Testament texts like Hebrews 1:5 possibly explains the origin of the term "person" in Christian theology. Although the Bible does not use the *term* "person" to describe the three agents of the one God's life, the Bible does engage in the *practice* of "person-centered" interpretation.[6] We will return to the Trinitarian concept of person in later chapters. For now, it is useful to have a label for that to which the Bible's Trinitarian discourse refers in proper predication.

---

6. Matthew W. Bates, *The Birth of the Trinity: Jesus, God, and the Spirit in New Testament and Early Christian Interpretation of the Old Testament* (Oxford: Oxford University Press, 2015).

Cosmic Framework Texts

Whereas inner-Trinitarian conversation texts focus primarily on relations between the persons of the Trinity, cosmic framework texts set the entire cosmos, as well as the entirety of God's work within the cosmos, in relation to the Trinity. Much as the hymnic account of creation in Genesis 1:1–2:3 functions in relation to the narrative account of creation in Genesis 2:4–25, these texts provide a cosmic framework within which the unfolding story of God's relation to his creatures becomes meaningful. Functioning like a playbill for a theatrical production, these texts identify characters and provide context for grasping the drama of creation, redemption, and consummation.

John 1:1–18 (John's "prologue") provides an entryway into John's larger narrative account of Jesus's life and ministry. It begins "in the beginning," before creation, portraying the Father and the Son existing in a stance of mutual repose and delight: "In the beginning was the Word, and the Word was facing God, and the Word was God" (John 1:1 ESV, altered). John's prologue concludes on the same note, portraying "the only begotten God" as leaning on "the Father's side" (John 1:18 ESV, altered).[7] The mutual love of the Father and the Son thus sets the context within which God's works of creation and redemption make sense.[8]

John 1:3–5 identifies the Word as the one through whom all things were made and as the life and light of men, which shines unconquered by the darkness of the cosmos. John 1:6–13 sets the work of "the true light" in contrast and relation to the witness of John the Baptist, identifying the latter as "a man sent from God" (v. 6) "to bear witness about the light" (v. 7). John

---

7. John 13:23 uses identical language to describe the beloved disciple reclining on Jesus's breast at the Last Supper.

8. Compare with John 17:24–26, which describes the mutual love and glory of the Father and the Son before the foundation of the world.

1:14–18 then describes the incarnation of the Word. The same Word who was with God in the beginning, through whom all things were made, becomes the means whereby God's redemptive purpose is fulfilled, causing those who receive him to become children of God, causing the fullness of God's grace and truth to dwell in our midst, declaring the glory of the unseen God. In each case, the incarnate Word transcends in his person and work what God did through Moses in ages past.

It is impossible to overestimate the significance of John 1:1–18 for Trinitarian theology. For now, let me simply summarize several relevant points. First, in a manner similar to Hebrews 1:5, this passage identifies the mutual love of the Father and the Son as the primary context for understanding the meaning and purpose of the cosmos (again, compare John 17:24–26). Second, this text at once distinguishes the Word from God and identifies the Word with God, thus exhibiting both proper predication and common predication, the basic grammar of the Bible's Trinitarian discourse. Third, this passage identifies the Word as the Creator of all things, placing him—with God—on the divine side of the distinction between Creator and creatures. Fourth, again in a manner similar to what we saw in Hebrews 1 with respect to angels, this text clearly distinguishes the Word from other messengers of God, in this case John the Baptist and Moses. Fifth, this passage identifies the Word as the divine agent of redemption who personally assumed our mortal nature ("flesh") to embrace us within God's family and to manifest God's invisible glory.

Colossians 1:15–20, like John 1:1–18, is a hymnic description of God's beloved Son (Col. 1:13) that frames the entirety of God's work in the cosmos in creation, redemption, and consummation in relation to him. Colossians 1:15 identifies God's beloved Son as "the image of the invisible God, the firstborn of all creation." The latter title extends to his status not only in relation to creation but also in relation to new creation: he is "the beginning, the firstborn from the dead" (Col. 1:18). Adopting a series of prepositions commonly used in ancient philosophical discussions of causality (e.g., "through," "in," "for"),[9] Colossians 1 describes God's beloved Son as the first and final cause of all creatures: "For by him all things were created, in heaven and on earth, visible and invisible, whether thrones or dominions or rulers or authorities—all things were created through him and for him" (v. 16). Colossians 1 also describes God's beloved Son as the cause of creation's providential harmony (v. 17) and as the cause of reconciliation, by means of his incarnation and bloody execution (vv. 19–20). Each description of God's beloved Son in turn aims at drawing our attention to one divine purpose for the cosmos: "that in everything he might be preeminent" (v. 18).

Again, like John 1:1–18, this cosmic-framework text sets all things in relation to God's beloved Son and to God's purpose in him. First, by means of proper predication, it identifies the second person of the Trinity as God's beloved Son and as the image of the invisible God. Second, it places the beloved Son on the divine side of the distinction between Creator and creatures. Third, it identifies him as the agent of creation, providence, and reconciliation. And, fourth, in each instance, it seeks to demonstrate the preeminence of Jesus Christ in all things, revealing a perspective on the relationship between the Son and creation that is similar to what we find in Hebrews 1.

Before moving on, we should note that, in both of the cosmic framework texts I have discussed, we hear echoes of Proverbs 8, as well other Jewish texts that reflect on God's Wisdom.

---

9. Compare this with Rom. 11:36's use of prepositions to describe the one God as the first and final cause of all things.

We will explore the significance of the Bible's identification of the Son with Wisdom in later chapters.

Redemptive Mission Texts

The final type of text we will consider in our survey of the Bible's Trinitarian discourse focuses on the sending or "mission" of the Son (and the Spirit) to fulfill God's redemptive purpose. Whereas inner-Trinitarian conversation texts focus on the relations between the persons of the Trinity, and whereas cosmic framework texts focus on the relation between the cosmos and the Trinity, "redemptive mission texts" focus on the one God's work of redemption and the relations between the persons in effecting that work of redemption. Two examples of this type of text will round out this discussion of the Bible and the Trinity.

In Mark 12:1–12, Jesus tells the parable of the tenants. This passage summarizes, in parable form, the main characters and plotline of Mark's Gospel as a whole. The parable portrays the Father as a man who plants a vineyard, Israel as that vineyard, and the leaders of Israel as tenants hired to keep the vineyard and to produce fruits for the owner. Time after time, the owner sends servants to collect the fruits of the vineyard. And, time after time, the tenants respond harshly to the owner's servants: some they beat, others they treat shamefully, still others they kill. At last, the owner of the vineyard sends his "beloved son" (Mark 12:6)—the same title applied to Jesus at his baptism and at his transfiguration (Mark 1:11; 9:7). The owner wagers, surely they will respect him. They, we know, do not. Instead, the tenants of the vineyard see the beloved son's appearance as their opportunity: "Those tenants said to one another, 'This is the heir. Come, let us kill him, and the inheritance will be ours'" (Mark 12:7). The tenants follow through with their wicked plot, taking the beloved son, killing him, and throwing him out of the vineyard.

But the story does not end there. Jesus asks and answers his own question: "What will the owner of the vineyard do? He will come and destroy the tenants and give the vineyard to others" (Mark 12:9). Jesus then quotes Psalm 118:22–23 to explain the ultimate narrative resolution to these events:

> The stone that the builders rejected
>   has become the cornerstone;
> this was the Lord's doing,
>   and it is marvelous in our eyes. (Mark 12:10–11)

The tenants' plot, far from undoing the beloved son's claim upon the vineyard, is the means of their own undoing, and the means whereby the beloved Son is established as the cornerstone of God's eschatological building (Eph. 2:20), in marvelous fulfillment of God's purpose.

Note several features of this passage. First, as in Colossians 1, the second person of the Trinity is portrayed as the special object of the Father's affection, as his "beloved son." Second, though he too is "sent" like the "servants" of the Father (undoubtedly a reference to Old Testament prophets), the second person of the Trinity is clearly distinguished from the servants of the Father, and that in two ways. On the one hand, the Son is sent at the climax of the story; the Father saves his best emissary for last (so John 1:15). On the other hand, the second person of the Trinity is aligned with the Father, being identified as co-owner of the vineyard, "the heir" (Mark 12:7), to whom its fruits are also rightly due. This is a powerful identification since much of the remainder of the chapter will be occupied with addressing the fruits that are due to the one God alone (Mark 12:13–17, 28–34).

In Galatians 4:4–7, Paul concludes an argument begun in chapter 3 regarding the identity of Abraham's true children and heirs. Having affirmed our baptismal status as "sons of God" (Gal. 3:26) and "Abraham's offspring, heirs according to promise" (Gal. 3:29), Paul recapitulates the means whereby our status as members of God's family has come about:

> But when the fullness of time had come, God sent forth his Son, born of woman, born under the law, to redeem those who were under the law, so that we might receive adoption as sons. And because you are sons, God has sent the Spirit of his Son into our hearts, crying, "Abba! Father!" So you are no longer a slave, but a son, and if a son, then an heir through God. (Gal. 4:4–7)

Again, several features of this text are worth noting. First, as in Mark 12:1–12, God saves his best emissary for last: "When the fullness of time had come, God sent forth his Son" (Gal. 4:4) to bring about an eschatological new exodus, redeeming us from slavery, securing our adoption, and assuring us that we will indeed arrive at our eschatological inheritance. Second, alongside the mission of God's "Son" (Gal. 4:4), Galatians 4:4–7 proclaims the mission of "the Spirit of his Son" (v. 6). Third, both missions, Paul insists, are included within the one saving agency of God. When God makes us heirs of God through the missions of the Son and the Spirit, he makes us heirs "through God" (v. 7), not through the agency of another (Hos. 1:7).

Fourth, Galatians 4:4–7 reveals how the relations that constitute the one God's life come to embrace us as well, to the praise of God's triune glory. God sends forth his divine Son to become incarnate and to redeem us in order that "we might receive adoption as sons" (v. 5). And God sends the Spirit of his

Son into our hearts to indwell us in order that the very cry of the divine Son to the divine Father might emerge from our hearts on our lips: "Abba! Father!" (v. 6). Here—gloriously—we see how the God who is Father, Son, and Spirit becomes our Father, through the Son, by the Spirit, making us sons of God by the incarnate Son of God, enabling us to enter into the Son's praise of the Father by the indwelling Spirit. The God who speaks to God within the life of the Trinity redeems and indwells us so that we too might speak to God in praise of the Trinity.

Conclusion: Summarizing the Biblical Doctrine of the Trinity

We conclude this chapter with a summary sketch of the Bible's teaching on the Trinity. Such a summary brings together much of what we have surveyed in this and the previous chapter. It also provides a foundation for the more thematic treatment of the doctrine of the Trinity in the chapters that follow. My hope is that it may also serve to further cultivate our fluency, as those baptized in the triune name, as we seek to read the Bible's Trinitarian discourse, to contemplate God's triune life, and to speak of and to the Trinity in prayer, proclamation, and praise.

1. There is one God, the source and end of all creatures.
2. The Father, the Son, and the Holy Spirit are identical with the one God and, as such, are on the divine side of the distinction between the one God and all creatures.
3. The Father, the Son, and the Holy Spirit are distinguished from each other only by relations of origin.
4. The relations of origin that distinguish the Father, the Son, and the Holy Spirit do not follow as a consequence of the one God's will to create. Rather, God's will to create follows the relations of origin that distinguish the Father, the Son, and the Holy Spirit.

5. Certain creatures are destined by God's grace to be embraced within the relations of the Father, the Son, and the Holy Spirit, to the praise of his triune glory.

6. God himself, through the missions of the Son and the Spirit, brings it about that certain creatures are embraced within the relations of the Father, the Son, and the Holy Spirit.

3

The Simplicity of God

Christian praise of the Trinity is praise of the one God. The oneness of God is intrinsic to the first and greatest commandment of the Old and New Testaments. Moses proclaims God's oneness and calls Israel to acknowledge God's singular worth by loving him with all their heart, soul, and might (Deut. 6:4–5). Jesus affirms God's oneness as "the most important" commandment of all (Mark 12:28–29) and says that a scribe's profession of God's oneness evidences his proximity to God's kingdom (Mark 12:34). Christians are baptized into "the name" of the one God (Matt. 28:19), and Christians confess the name of the one God (1 Cor. 8:6). "The LORD is one" (Deut. 6:4).

The Christian doctrine of the Trinity is teaching about the one God, the author and end of all things; about the relations between the Father, the Son, and the Holy Spirit that constitute the one God's inner life; and about the manner in which the one God extends those relations to his people through his works of creation, redemption, and consummation, to the praise of his glory. Christian teaching about the one God includes teaching about his "unity of singularity" and teaching about his "unity of simplicity."[1] God's unity of singularity means that God alone is God and there are no other gods but God. God's unity of simplicity means that God is one with himself, selfsame and indivisible in his being and operations, and God is not composed of parts. God is pure God, and nothing but God is God.[2]

It is tempting to think that the doctrine of the Trinity is concerned only with God's "threeness" and not with God's oneness. But to succumb to this temptation would be a terrible mistake. The doctrine of divine unity in general and the doctrine of divine simplicity in particular are central to an orthodox Christian confession of the Trinity. The doctrine of divine simplicity further elucidates the basic grammar of the Bible's Trinitarian discourse by helping us better appreciate the kind of oneness that characterizes God's triune life, by helping us more deeply affirm the full divinity of the persons of the Trinity, and by helping us better grasp what distinguishes the persons of the Trinity from each other.

The purpose of this chapter is to unpack the preceding claims regarding the simplicity of the triune God. First, we will consider the meaning of the doctrine of divine simplicity. Second, we will consider the significance of the doctrine of divine simplicity for the doctrine of the Trinity.

Simplicity

"This is the message we have heard from him and proclaim to you, that God is light, and in him is no darkness at all" (1 John 1:5). This truth, taught by Jesus, heard by John, and proclaimed to us in apostolic writing, summarizes basic Christian teaching about divine simplicity. God is identical with light, and God is

---

1. Herman Bavinck, *Reformed Dogmatics*, ed. John Bolt, trans. John Vriend, vol. 2, *God and Creation* (Grand Rapids, MI: Baker Academic, 2004), 170.

2. Paraphrasing William Desmond: "God is God and nothing but God is God" (Desmond, *God and the Between* [Oxford: Blackwell, 2008], 50).

nothing but light. The truth taught in this verse also exhibits the basic grammar of divine simplicity, providing us with a "standard" (Rom. 6:17) or "pattern" (2 Tim. 1:13) to guide our thinking and speaking about the simple God. God is identical with his perfection, and he is wholly perfection, without any mixture of imperfection. He is wisdom, and in him is no folly at all. He is goodness, and in him is no evil at all. He is power, and in him is no weakness at all. He is being, and in him is no nonbeing, no unfulfilled being at all.

The identity of God with God, and the lack of all composition in God, is what Christians affirm when they confess the doctrine of divine simplicity. Johannes Wollebius (1589–1629) offers a representative summary of Christian teaching on divine simplicity that can help us further appreciate the meaning of the doctrine. According to Wollebius, to confess a simple, non-composite God is to say, "He is not compounded of parts, or of genus and species [differentia], or of substance and accidents, or of potentiality and act, or of being and essence."[3]

God is not composed of parts. Unlike human beings, God is not a composite of body and soul. God is spirit, not flesh (Isa. 31:3). Nor is God composed of metaphysical parts. God is not part light and part darkness, part this and part that. God is pure and unmixed light (1 John 1:5), pure and unmixed being, pure and unmixed wisdom, pure and unmixed goodness, pure and unmixed power. Divine simplicity, thus understood, follows from divine spirituality—"God is spirit" (John 4:24).

God is not composed of genus and species. As we saw in an earlier chapter, there is no larger category of gods of which

3. Johannes Wollebius, *Compendium Theologiae Christianae*, in *Reformed Dogmatics: J. Wollebius, G. Voetius, F. Turretin*, ed. John W. Beardslee (Eugene, OR: Wipf & Stock, 2009), 39.

the Lord is a member. "YHWH is *the* God" (Deut. 4:35, my trans.). Nor do God and creatures together compose a larger category of things (beings, persons, etc.) of which God is a greater version and creatures are lesser versions. God is not just a greater version of this or that kind of thing. The God who created all things transcends the categories of all created things. Indeed, he transcends categorization altogether. Divine simplicity, thus understood, follows from God's transcendent, categorical uniqueness (Ps. 135:5; Isa. 40:18). God is the incomparable one.

God is not composed of substance and accidents. God does not have attributes in the way we have attributes. We possess specific attributes or qualities, such as wisdom or brown hair, that are metaphysically distinct from ourselves. We can grow or decrease in wisdom or lack wisdom altogether. Yet we still remain who we are as wiser, less wise, or unwise versions of ourselves. The color of our hair can change, or our hair can fall out altogether. Yet we still remain who we are. Many of our qualities and attributes do not inhere in us essentially. To be Scott is not *essentially* to be right-handed. To be Scott is not *essentially* to have brown hair, or even to have hair at all. Not so with God. God is identical with the perfections we attribute to him. God *is* light (1 John 1:5). God *is* love (1 John 4:8). God *is* the truth. God *is* the life (John 14:6). Who God is and what God is are identical. He is who he is (Ex. 3:14). This is divine simplicity in the strict and proper sense. God is the great "I AM."

God is not composed of potentiality and act. Unlike creatures, in God there is no potential for growth, diminishment, or change (Ps. 102:25–27). God does not gain or lose perfection (Job 22:2–3; 35:6–7; 41:11; Rom. 11:33, 35). God is not metaphysically divisible from what he once was or what he one day will become. He is "the same" yesterday, today, and forever (Heb. 13:8), the one "who was and is and is to come" (Rev. 4:8). With him "there is no variation or shadow due to change" (James 1:17). Divine simplicity, thus understood, follows from divine immutability. God is the selfsame one.

God is not composed of being and essence. What a creature is (e.g., a dog, a cat, a snake) and *that* a creature is are metaphysically distinct. What a creature is does not entail its existence. In fact, we can imagine many kinds of creatures (e.g., unicorns, leprechauns) that do not in fact exist. Not so with God. *What* God is and *that* God is are identical. He is "the one who is" (see Ex. 3:14 LXX; Rev. 4:8), the consuming fire who does not rely on any fuel outside himself in order to burn (Ex. 3:2–3). God has "life in himself" (John 5:26). Divine simplicity, thus understood, follows from divine self-existence. God is the self-existent one.

As the preceding discussion suggests, divine simplicity is not merely one divine attribute among many within the Christian doctrine of God. The attribute of divine simplicity is paradigmatic, the basic grammar of God's proper name, YHWH, as revealed by God in Exodus 3:14: "I AM WHO I AM." Divine simplicity describes how the one God has attributes. And divine simplicity, in turn, is described by describing the one God's other attributes (e.g., spirituality, uniqueness, immutability, self-existence). Such a situation is just what we might expect when it comes to describing the one and simple God.

The doctrine of divine simplicity not only helps us better appreciate the oneness of God in his being and attributes. It also helps us better appreciate what it means for the one God to be the author and end of all things, the first and the last (Rev. 22:13).

All composition presupposes a composer. That a creature exists—and that a creature exists as a particular kind of creature instead of another kind of creature—depends upon God alone. He alone calls all creatures into existence, causing them to be what they are and causing it to be that they are (Gen. 1:3–31). But no one and no thing causes the one God to be who, what, or that he is. Who has caused him to exist? Who has taught him wisdom (Rom. 11:34)? Who has ever given anything to him (Rom. 11:35)? The answer to all of these questions is "no one." Lacking a composer, God—the first cause—lacks all composition. He is the *self*-existent, *self*-wise, *self*-good, *self*-powerful God: "From him and through him and to him are all things. To him be glory forever" (Rom. 11:36).[4]

In similar fashion, God's identity as the final hope of his people, their supreme blessing and reward, is further illumined and underlined by the doctrine of divine simplicity. The supreme goods that God has promised us in Christ are not finally divisible from God himself. The true food for which the human soul hungers, the true drink for which the human soul thirsts is not merely something that God gives. It is something that God himself is. Our souls long for the living God (Ps. 42:2). He *is* the bread of life, the soul's true food, the soul's true drink (John 6:35). The one and simple God, the final cause of all creatures, is himself the soul's reward (Rev. 21:7).

The last thing to note here is that, because the one God is simple, all of the one God's external works are indivisible, undivided. God alone created all things (Isa. 44:24), and God alone is our Redeemer (Hos. 1:7). God's transcendent oneness

---

4. The doctrine of divine simplicity thus rules out the perennial philosophical mistake of thinking either that God required help in causing all things to be or that God needed to look to something outside himself after which to pattern various creaturely kinds and perfections. Quite to the contrary, the doctrine of divine simplicity teaches us that God *himself* is the sole cause of the existence and essence of all creatures (Isa. 44:24; Rom. 11:36; Eph. 3:14–15).

thus not only shapes our understanding of God's being; it also shapes our understanding of God's works. Because of divine simplicity, the external works of the triune God are not parceled out among the persons, with each person perhaps doing his share to contribute to a larger whole. The external works of the triune God are indivisible. All of God's works, from creation to consummation, are works of the three persons enacting one divine power, ordered by one divine wisdom, expressing one divine goodness, and manifesting one divine glory. We will return to this important principle in later chapters when considering the nature of God's external works.

Simplicity and Trinity

The Bible's basic Trinitarian grammar affirms the oneness of God, identifies the three persons of the Trinity with the one God, and distinguishes the three persons of the Trinity by their relations of origin. We have already seen how the doctrine of divine simplicity further illumines the first element of the Bible's Trinitarian grammar by helping us appreciate the character of God's transcendent oneness. Let us now consider how it further illumines the other two elements of the Bible's basic Trinitarian grammar.

The Bible identifies the three persons of the Trinity with the one God. Given the character of God's oneness as expressed in the doctrine of divine simplicity, we may rule out two Trinitarian errors. First, the three persons of the Trinity should not be considered three "parts" of the Trinity, each person being one third of God that, when added together, "compose" God as a whole. Such a view fails for the simple reason that the one God has no parts. The Father, the Son, and the Spirit are not parts of the one God. Each person is the one God in all his fullness (Col. 1:19; 2:9). The Father is the one God in all his fullness.

The Son is the one God in all his fullness. The Spirt is the one God in all his fullness.

Second, the three persons of the Trinity are not instances of a larger category of being that we call "God." Here the distinction between the one God and creatures shines forth. "Humanity," as a category of being, is divided among the many individual human beings that instantiate human nature. Each human being is an individual version of the thing that human beings are. To multiply human persons is, of necessity, to multiply human beings. Two human persons add up to two human beings, two human minds, two human wills, two human powers, and so forth. Not so when it comes to the one God, for the simple reason that the one God is not composed of genus and species. The one God is indivisible. And so to affirm that the three persons of the Trinity are the one God is not to affirm the existence of three gods. The multiplication of divine persons within the one God does not amount to the multiplication of divine beings, divine minds, divine wills, or divine powers. In the one God all of these things—the divine being, the divine mind, the divine will, and the divine power—are one and indivisible. For us there is one God, one Lord, one Spirit (1 Cor. 8:6; Eph. 4:4–6).

Contrary to these errors, and stated positively, the grammar of divine simplicity requires us to affirm that each divine person is identical with the one God in all his fullness. There is nothing that the Father is that the Son and the Spirit are not, except for being the Father. There is nothing that the Son is that the Father and the Spirit are not, except for being the Son. And there is nothing that the Spirit is that the Father and the Son are not, except for being the Spirit. The time-honored way of summarizing the point is this: in God all things are one where no relation of opposition (i.e., the relations of origin that distinguish the persons) intervenes.[5] That is to say, each divine person is equally and identically the one true and living God; the only real distinctions between the persons are their relations to each other (on which, see below). This leads us to the relationship between divine simplicity and the last element of the Bible's basic Trinitarian grammar.

The doctrine of divine simplicity not only clarifies the character of God's transcendent oneness and not only clarifies what it means to identify the three persons of the Trinity with the one God; it also clarifies the nature of the distinctions that exist between the persons of the Trinity within the one God. How so?

The answer lies in recalling once again the way the Bible distinguishes the persons of the Trinity from each other: by means of their relations of origin. The Father eternally begets the Son ("paternity") and the Son is eternally begotten of the Father ("filiation"). The Father and the Son eternally breathe forth the Spirit ("active spiration," i.e., breathing forth), and the Spirit is eternally breathed forth by the Father and the Son ("passive spiration," i.e., being breathed forth).

According to the Bible's basic Trinitarian grammar, these relations of origin, and the "personal properties" that label them (paternity, filiation, spiration), are the only real distinctions that exist within the one and simple God. The Father is not the Son. The Son is not the Father. The Spirit is not the Father or the Son. While these distinct personal ways of being the one God require absolutely no distinction between the persons of the Trinity and the one God, thus preserving divine simplicity, they also exhibit how the persons of the Trinity are truly distinct from each other—by the manner in which they communicate God's simple essence to each other: "As the Father has life in

---

5. Anselm, *On the Procession of the Holy Spirit*, 1, in *Anselm of Canterbury: The Major Works* (Oxford: Oxford University Press, 2008), 393, 396.

himself, so he has granted the Son also to have life in himself" (John 5:26). The person of the Father eternally communicates his simple essence to the person of the Son in eternal generation. In similar fashion, just as the Father and the Son have life in themselves, so they have granted the Spirit to have life in himself. The persons of the Father and the Son eternally communicate their simple essence to the Spirit in eternal spiration.

The relations of origin thus preserve the perfect simplicity of God's triune life, even as they manifest the perfect fecundity of God's triune life. The simple God is no dry fountain, no dead spring. God's life is indivisible, but it is not incommunicable. The simple God is the eternal life of communication and communion that is the Father, the Son, and the Holy Spirit, the blessed Trinity. Or, to put the matter in its native biblical idiom, "God *is* light" (1 John 1:5), simple and indivisible. And "God is *light*" (1 John 1:5), internally fruitful in the persons of the Father, the Son, and the Holy Spirit. The Father's simple light shines forth in the radiance of his Son (Heb. 1:3) and in the Spirit who alights on them both in their mutual love. God "dwells in unapproachable light" (1 Tim. 6:16), the Father resting in the Son by the Spirit (Luke 3:22), and the Son rejoicing in the Father by the same Spirit (Luke 10:21).

Conclusion

In this chapter we have seen that the doctrine of divine simplicity further illumines the Bible's basic Trinitarian grammar by illumining the character of God's transcendent oneness, the identity of the three persons of the Trinity with the one God, and the real distinctions that exist between the persons of the Trinity within the one God. In so doing, we have glimpsed more of the beauty of God's triune life in its transcendent simplicity and radiant splendor.

And, to the extent that we have done so, we must consider our analysis a success. The reason for attending to the Bible's Trinitarian discourse, and for disciplining our minds and lips before the radiance of God's simple light, is not to explain God's triune life but to stand in awe of it, to adore it, and to embrace it as it unfolds itself to us in Scripture. "Hear, O Israel: The LORD our God, the LORD is one. You shall love the LORD your God with all your heart and with all your soul and with all your might" (Deut. 6:4–5).

Nevertheless, while we cannot hope to comprehend the wonder of God's triune life, we can press more deeply into the Bible's Trinitarian discourse. Because the revelation of God's triune name is pleasant (Ps. 135:3), we can savor it at length and, in so doing, taste and see further dimensions of the Lord's transcendent goodness (Ps. 34:8). This we will do in the chapters that follow, savoring, tasting, and, by God's grace, glimpsing further dimensions of the Lord's transcendent goodness as Father, Son, and Holy Spirit.

4

God the Father

Christian praise of the triune God includes praise of God the Father. Paul begins his letter to the Ephesians with praise of the Father's name: "Blessed be the God and Father of our Lord Jesus Christ, who has blessed us in Christ with every spiritual blessing in the heavenly places" (1:3). In blessing "the God and Father of our Lord Jesus Christ," Paul names the first person of the Trinity by means of his relation to the second person of the Trinity: the first person is Jesus's Father; the second person (Jesus) is the Father's Son.

Paul's praise of the Father does not end there. The apostle praises God the Father of our Lord Jesus Christ for fathering us (via adoption) in and through Jesus Christ (Eph. 1:5–6) and for sealing us with his Spirit for the day when we will receive our final redemption and full inheritance (Eph. 1:13–14). He thereby also names God *our* Father in and through his Son by the Spirit. These blessings, in turn, not only prompt the praise of the Father's glorious grace (Eph. 1:6, 12, 14). They also reveal the Father's ultimate purpose of exalting the name of Jesus Christ, his beloved Son, "above every name that is named, not only in this age but also in the one to come" (Eph. 1:21; see also 1:9–10, 20–23). The praise of the Father's name thus embraces his relation to the Son and, in and through the Son and the Spirit, his relation to us, to the mutual glory of the Father and the Son in the Spirit (Eph. 5:18–19).

In Ephesians 3:14–15, Paul further expands his praise of God the Father, addressing him as "the Father, from whom every family in heaven and on earth is named." And in Ephesians 4:6, at the climax of a triadic formula (Eph. 4:4–6), Paul blesses "one God and Father of all, who is over all and through all and in all." The praise of the Father's name, according to Ephesians, thus includes the Father's relation to the Son, the Father's relation to his redeemed children in the Son, and the Father's relation to all things in heaven and on earth. The rest of the Bible echoes Ephesians' threefold praise of the Father's name as well, acknowledging him to be the Father of his only begotten Son (John 1:18; 3:16; Heb. 1:5), the Father of all creatures (James 1:17), and the Father of Jesus's redeemed siblings (John 1:12; Gal. 4:6).

In turning to consider the Father's name, we turn from consideration of the one God's simplicity to consideration of his tripersonal fecundity or fruitfulness. As we saw in the conclusion of the previous chapter, the one God's simple light shines forth in tripersonal glory: shining forth *from* the person of the Father, shining *in* the person of the Son, and shining *upon* both the Father and the Son in the person of the Spirit. In the persons of the Father, the Son, and the Holy Spirit, "the blessed and only Sovereign" "dwells in unapproachable light" (1 Tim. 6:15–16).

Now we must add that the divine light that shines forth within God's tripersonal life also shines forth outside of God's tripersonal life in God's works of creation, redemption, and consummation. God is not only internally fruitful and productive; he is externally fruitful and productive as well. God is "the Father of lights, with whom there is no variation or shadow due to change," the source of "every good and perfect gift" in creation and new creation. "Of his own will he brought us forth by the word of truth, that we should be a kind of firstfruits of his creatures" (James 1:17–18).

The purpose of the present chapter is to honor the Father's name by considering the manifold ways in which the Bible's Trinitarian discourse manifests the Father's fecundity. Our discussion will proceed as follows: I will first outline the basic grammar of the Bible's naming of God the Father. We will then reflect more deeply upon biblical naming of God the Father, considering the nature of God's fatherhood in its primacy, uniqueness, and transcendence, as well as the nature of language regarding God's fatherhood. Attending to the biblical naming of God the Father under both headings will help us better appreciate not only how the Bible speaks about the first person of the Trinity but also how it speaks about the second and third persons of the Trinity, as well as how it speaks about the triune God's external works in creation, redemption, and consummation.

Naming God the Father: The Basic Grammar

In previous chapters we had opportunity to consider a distinction fundamental to the Bible's basic Trinitarian grammar, the distinction between "common predication" and "proper predication." Common predication refers to what the three persons hold in common as the one and simple God: they share the one God's holy name, YHWH, one divine being, one divine wisdom, one divine goodness, and one divine power. In contrast to common predication, proper predication refers to what each person of the Trinity holds in distinction from the other two persons. The "personal properties" of paternity, filiation, and spiration identify that which foundationally and fundamentally distinguishes the persons of the Trinity: the Father eternally begets the Son (paternity), the Son is eternally begotten of the Father (filiation), and the Father and the Son eternally breathe forth the Spirit (spiration).

This basic grammar can be further sharpened and clarified in light of the Bible's threefold naming of the Father. As we saw above, the Bible calls God Father both to describe relations that are *internal* to the Trinity, and thus *identical* with the one God's life, and to describe relations that are *external* to the Trinity, and thus *not identical* with the one God's life. The Father's relation to the Son is internal to the one God, and both the Father and the Son are identical with the one God. The Father's relation to creation as a whole, in general, and to his redeemed people, in particular, is not internal to the one God's life, nor are any of God's creatures identical with the one God. God could and would be Father apart from creating or redeeming us. And, for all the intimacy we enjoy with the triune God as his redeemed children, we will always remain creatures.

How does the Bible's threefold way of naming God the Father further clarify the distinction between common and proper naming? When the Bible calls God the Father of his beloved Son, it engages in proper predication. In this application, the name "Father" is *exclusively* predicated of the first person of the Trinity. The Father *alone* eternally begets the Son. However, when the Bible calls God the Father of all creatures or the Father of his redeemed children, it engages in common predication. Any time the Bible predicates a relationship between God the Father and his creatures, in nature and in grace, it always *includes* (at least indirectly) reference to the Son and the Spirit. Why is that? Because *all* of God's external works in creation, redemption, and consummation are indivisible operations of the Trinity, proceeding from the Father, through the Son, in the Spirit. Does the Bible attribute creation to the Father? It does (1 Cor. 8:6; Eph. 3:9; James 3:17), but never in such a way as to exclude the Son and the Spirit, because the Father creates through the Son by the Spirit (Gen. 1; Ps. 33:6; 1 Cor. 8:6). Does the Bible attribute redemption to the Father? The answer again is affirmative (John 3:16; Rom. 8:32), but the Bible never does so in a way that excludes the Son and the Spirit, because the Father redeems us through the Son by the Spirit (2 Cor. 8:9; Gal. 2:20; 4:4–7; Heb. 9:14).

We will return to this particular refinement of the Bible's Trinitarian grammar in later chapters when I address God's external works in greater detail. For now, it is enough to observe that biblical naming of the Father follows two distinct patterns of predication: one that refers *exclusively* to the Father as the first person of the Trinity in distinction from the Son and the Spirit, another that refers *inclusively* to the Father as the first person of the Trinity, embracing the persons of the Son and the Spirit as well in all references to the Trinity's undivided external works.

Naming God the Father: Primacy, Uniqueness, and Transcendence

Our Lord Jesus taught us to sanctify the Father's name in prayer:

> Our Father in heaven,
> hallowed be your name. (Matt. 6:9)

Accordingly, the goal of Christian theology is to gain greater fluency in biblical discourse, that we might more faithfully hallow the Father's name in prayer, proclamation, and praise. Learning to hallow the Father's name in its threefold biblical significance requires us to reflect a bit more deeply on the similarities and dissimilarities between God's fatherhood and all other forms of fatherhood. As we will see, the fatherhood of God is primary, unique, and transcendent,[1] and this, in turn, determines how we should think about what it means to hallow the Father's name in human language.

First, the fatherhood of God is primary. The fatherhood of God is the first form of fatherhood, preexisting all other creaturely forms of fatherhood. Before the existence of creation, and thus before the existence of creaturely fathers and creaturely sons, the Father and his only begotten Son dwelled in eternal, mutual delight in the fellowship of the Holy Spirit (John 1:1; 17:24–26). Moreover, just as God's fatherhood is primary in the order of being, so also is it primary in the order of meaning. Every creaturely fatherhood in heaven and on earth is patterned after his divine fatherhood, not vice versa. He is "the Father, from whom every family in heaven and on earth is named" (Eph. 3:14–15). All creaturely fatherhood is an image and likeness of his divine fatherhood (Gen. 5:1–3).

Second, therefore, the fatherhood of God is unique. The fatherhood of God is not modeled after the fatherhood of creatures. Nor does the fatherhood of God belong to a larger class of fatherhood of which divine fatherhood and creaturely fatherhood are members. God's fatherhood is holy, set apart, and singular. It is the fatherhood of the one God. Its meaning, therefore, is not defined by the measure of creaturely forms of fatherhood or by some generic sense of fatherhood that might apply to both God and man. The meaning of God's fatherhood is determined by God's fatherhood alone. He is who he is (Ex. 3:14). His fatherhood is one (1 Cor. 8:6; Eph. 4:6).

---

1. Gregory of Nazianzus, *Oration* 28.31, in *On God and Christ: The Five Theological Orations and Two Letters to Cledonius* (Crestwood, NY: St Vladimir's Seminary Press, 2002), 64.

Third, therefore, the fatherhood of God is transcendent. Because the fatherhood of God is primary, first in the order of being and first in the order of meaning, and because the fatherhood of God is unique, determined by God's fatherhood alone and not by any external standard of fatherhood, the fatherhood of God transcends all creaturely limitations. Unlike the fatherhood of creatures, the fatherhood of God is not dependent, not composite, not changing, not limited, and not temporal. It is self-existent, simple, immutable, infinite, and eternal. God's radiant fatherhood is "above" all other forms of fatherhood; he is "the Father of lights, with whom there is no variation or shadow due to change" (James 1:17).

The preceding discussion helps us appreciate why there is a family resemblance between God's fatherhood and creaturely forms of fatherhood—the latter are patterned after the former. It also helps us appreciate why there can be no one-to-one comparison between God's fatherhood and creaturely forms of fatherhood—God's fatherhood is unique and transcendent.

The above discussion also helps us appreciate something regarding the *language* we use in speaking of God's fatherhood. When God the Father reveals himself through the Son and by the Spirit in Holy Scripture, he stoops down and takes our language on his lips. He does not speak to us in the language of angels. He speaks to us in the language of human beings, "as a man" (Deut. 1:31; 8:5). Moreover, in doing so, the Father invites us to take his holy name upon our lips using language native to the children of men. And so we cry, "Abba! Father!" (Gal. 4:6), taking on our lips terms originally written in Aramaic and Greek.

The Father loves his children and therefore condescends to speak to them in the language of his children, and he invites them to speak to him in their own language as well. That said, we should not take the Father's gracious condescension to speak to us in our language as evidence that God's fatherhood is an instance of creaturely fatherhood. But neither should we consider this child's play—as if God were uttering empty syllables without transcendent significance.

When the Bible speaks of God the Father using ordinary human language, and when we, following the Bible's lead, call upon God the Father in the ordinary human language of prayer, proclamation, and praise, we speak in an *analogical* manner. We do not speak in a *univocal* manner—that is, predicating the same things of God's fatherhood that we predicate of creaturely forms of fatherhood—because God's fatherhood is unique and transcendent. Nor do we speak in an *equivocal* manner—that is, predicating absolutely different things of God's fatherhood than we predicate of creaturely forms of fatherhood—because creaturely forms of fatherhood were made to resemble, in some distant way, God's unique and transcendent fatherhood. Rather, we speak analogically, acknowledging both similarity and dissimilarity between God's fatherhood and all creaturely forms of fatherhood.[2]

In speaking analogically of God the Father, we acknowledge that God is truly Father—in relation to his only begotten Son and in relation to us as our Maker and Redeemer. We also acknowledge that he is Father in a primary, unique, and transcendent sense, in a manner that finally exceeds all comprehension (Ps. 145:3) and all speech (Neh. 9:5). He is "our Father *in heaven*" (Matt. 6:9), a name so wonderful that it is best hallowed in praise: "Blessed be the God and Father of our Lord Jesus Christ" (Eph. 1:3).

---

2. For further discussion of this important topic, see Steven J. Duby, "To Whom Will You Compare Me? Retrieving the (Right) Doctrine of Analogy," in *God in Himself: Scripture, Metaphysics, and the Task of Christian Theology* (Downers Grove, IL: IVP Academic, 2019).

The significance of analogical language for Trinitarian theology will become clearer in the next chapter when we consider the nature of divine "persons."

Conclusion

The name "Father" manifests the one God's fecundity or fruitfulness within himself and outside himself. The Father's fecundity shines in relations that are internal and identical with the life of the one God, in eternally begetting his radiant Son, and, with the Son, in eternally breathing forth his blessed Spirit. The Father's fecundity shines in relations that are external and nonidentical with the life of the one God in the undivided works of the Trinity that flow from the Father through the Son in the Spirit, producing all things out of nothing, preserving them from day to day, graciously redeeming a people for himself, bringing that redeemed people—in and with a new creation—to the glory appointed for them from before the foundation of the world, and summing up all things in heaven and on earth under the head of his beloved Son, to the glory of God the Father.

The glory of God the Father, both in himself and outside himself, is thus always exhibited in the glory of God the Son by the glory of God the Spirit. And this is what we should expect when attending to the glory of the one God's simple and fecund life: the glory of the one God is essentially tripersonal, essentially relational. In the chapters that follow, we turn to the glory of the Father as it shines in the face of Jesus Christ, as it alights upon Jesus Christ in the Spirit, and as it manifests itself in the works of nature, grace, and glory, to the praise of the blessed Trinity.

5

God the Son

Christians give praise to God the Father and, with him, to God the Son:

> To him who sits on the throne and to the Lamb
> be blessing and honor and glory and might forever and
> ever! (Rev. 5:13)

In the Son, the radiance of the Father's glory eternally shines forth: The Son is the Father's eternal Word and image, the exact imprint of his being (John 1:1; Col. 1:15; Heb. 1:3). On the Son, the good pleasure of the Father eternally rests: The Father loved the Son before the foundation of the world (John 17:24). The Father delighted in the Son when the world was brought into being (Prov. 8:30). The Father declared his pleasure in the Son at his baptism and transfiguration (Mark 1:11; 9:7). The Father loves the Son because he laid down his life for his sheep (John 10:17). And, because of his obedience unto death, the Father enthroned the Son forever at his right hand, the seat of divine fullness of joy and pleasures forevermore (Ps. 16:11; Phil. 2:6–11). Through and for the Son all things were created,

and through and for the Son all that will be redeemed will
be redeemed (Col. 1:15–20; Heb. 1:1–4). The gospel is about
him: his birth, his death, his resurrection, and his glory (Rom.
1:1–7; 1 Cor. 15:3–4). The nations are his inheritance, as are
heaven and earth and all that is in them (Ps. 2:8; Heb. 1:2).
The church is his bride (Eph. 5:22–33). The ultimate end in
the Father's sending of the Son is "that all may honor the Son,
just as they honor the Father" (John 5:23), that the Son might
have preeminence in all things (Col. 1:18). Accordingly, when
the Son is acclaimed as Lord, the Father is glorified (Phil. 2:11).

In the previous chapter, we considered the biblical grammar of divine naming with respect to God the Father, the first
person of the Trinity. We also contemplated what it means to
honor the Father's name in its primacy, uniqueness, and transcendence. Building on that discussion, we will consider here
what it means to honor the Son's name just as we honor the
Father's name (John 5:23).

As we will see more fully below, the church honors the
name of the Son by confessing that he is "begotten, not made,
consubstantial with the Father."[1] When Christians confess that
the Son of God is "begotten, not made," they acknowledge
that what personally distinguishes the Father from the Son
is categorically different from what distinguishes God from
creatures. The relationship between the Father who begets and
the Son who is begotten is a relationship between divine persons, not between a divine producer and a creaturely product.
Moreover, far from dividing God's simple being, in the Father's
eternal begetting of the Son, the Father eternally communicates
his simple being to the Son: "As the Father has life in himself,
so he has granted the Son also to have life in himself" (John
5:26). Christians thus confess not only that the Son of God

---

1. Nicene-Constantinopolitan Creed (AD 381).

is "begotten, not made" but also that he is "consubstantial with the Father"—one with the Father in his being, attributes, works, and worship.

As we will also see more fully below, there are alternative ways of describing the person of the Son that inevitably dishonor his name, either by denying the Son's distinct personhood, diminishing the Son's deity, or by dividing God's simple being. Because the glory of Jesus Christ is at stake, errors here are treacherous.

Naming God the Son

We saw in the previous chapter that Scripture manifests a threefold naming of God the Father. He is described as the Father of our Lord Jesus Christ (Eph. 1:3), the Father of Jesus's redeemed siblings (Eph. 1:5), and the Father of all creatures (Eph. 3:14–15). Note that there are certain family resemblances between each of these Father-child relations. In each instance, we are dealing with two distinct terms of the relation: the Father and the Son, in the first instance; the Father and the redeemed, in the second instance; and the Father and his creatures, in the third instance. Moreover, in each instance, the Father is the originator of the relationship between the two distinct terms of the relation: the Father eternally begets the Son; the Father adopted Jesus's redeemed siblings; the Father created all things. Though these family resemblances are real, there are some very real differences between the Father-Son relation and the various Father-creature relations as well. And if we fail to note these differences, we will fail to honor the Son as he deserves. What is the nature of the differences? As mentioned above, the Son is "begotten, not made." The relation between the Father and the Son is a relation between divine persons, not between a divine producer and a creaturely product.

Our earlier survey of the Bible's Trinitarian discourse confirms this point. Scripture identifies the Son as a divine person (as opposed to a creaturely product) by means of various personal names and titles. Employing "prosopological exegesis" of Psalm 2:7, Hebrews 1:5 identifies the second person of the Trinity as God's "Son," eternally begotten of the Father. John 1:1, Colossians 1:15, and Hebrews 1:3 further illumine the identity of the second person of the Trinity by describing him as God's eternal "Word," "image," and "radiance." These personal names and titles identify the second person of the Trinity by means of his mutual, asymmetrical relation to the first person of the Trinity. The second person of the Trinity is the Son, eternally begotten of the Father; the Word, eternally uttered by the Father; the image, perfectly representing the Father; the radiance, eternally shining forth from the Father. Moreover, all these personal names and titles locate the second person of the Trinity on the divine side of the Creator-creature distinction. The Father's Son, Word, image, and radiance is the one through whom and for whom all creatures exist and, therefore, to whom their worship is due.

Inasmuch as the Son is "begotten, not made," the sonship (or "filiation") of the second person of the Trinity, like the fatherhood (or "paternity") of the first person of the Trinity, is primary, unique, and transcendent. The sonship of the second person of the Trinity is primary. He is the Father's "firstborn" Son (Rom. 8:29; Col. 1:15; Heb. 1:6), whose birth in Bethlehem is preceded by his birth in eternity (Mic. 5:2), before God created all things (Prov. 8:22–31; John 1:1). And, as his sonship is first in the order of being, it is also first in the order of meaning. All other sons, whether in creation or redemption, come into being through him and for him, being in some sense fashioned after his divine filial likeness (John 1:3, 11–13; Rom. 8:29;

Col. 1:15). Indeed, he is the divine light and life after which all creaturely light and life are patterned and in whose presence their meaning and purpose are revealed (Ps. 36:9; John 1:3; 8:12; 14:6).

Because it is first in the order of being and meaning, the sonship of the second person of the Trinity is also unique. In Johannine idiom, he is the "only begotten Son" (John 1:14, 18; 3:16 ESV, altered), while all others are "children" (John 1:12).[2] The eternal begetting of the Son therefore cannot be subsumed under or contemplated as an instance of creaturely modes of begetting, and every attempt to do so inevitably compromises the Son's uniqueness and incomparability (1 Sam. 2:2; Isa. 40:18).

Primary and unique, the sonship of the second person of the Trinity is also transcendent. All creatures have a beginning and an end. All creatures change through seasons of growth and decay, composition and decomposition. But the Son remains the same. His years have no beginning, and they have no end (Heb. 1:5, 10–12). Before all creatures and above all creatures, the only begotten Son of God lives and reigns eternal and unchanging, "the same yesterday and today and forever" (Heb. 13:8; see also Ps. 110; John 8:58). The eternal begetting of the Son thus transcends all manner of creaturely begetting: it is incomprehensible, timeless, indivisible, and impassible.[3]

With the primacy, uniqueness, and transcendence of the only begotten Son in view, we can better appreciate a distinctive feature of the Bible's Trinitarian discourse. In presenting the second person of the Trinity to us, Scripture uses a combination of social and psychological analogies. On the one hand,

---

2. For this translation of the Greek term *monogenēs*, see Charles Lee Irons, "A Lexical Defense of the Johannine 'Only-Begotten,'" in *Retrieving Eternal Generation*, ed. Fred Sanders and Scott R. Swain (Grand Rapids, MI: Zondervan Academic, 2017).

3. Petrus van Mastricht, *Theoretical-Practical Theology*, trans. Todd M. Rester, vol. 2 (Grand Rapids, MI: Reformation Heritage, 2019), 547–48.

the relation between the first and second persons of the Trinity is often portrayed, by means of social analogies, as a relation between a "father" and a "son." On the other hand, drawing upon Old Testament and Jewish imagery connected to divine Wisdom, the relation between the first and second persons of the Trinity is often portrayed, by means of psychological analogies, as a relation that is internal to God's being—that is, the relation between God and his own Word, image, and radiance. Furthermore, both kinds of analogies often occur together in the same scriptural contexts (e.g., John 1:1–18; Col. 1:15–20; Heb. 1:1–4).

We are tempted to ask, which is it? Is the relation between the first and second persons of the Trinity more like a relation between two distinct agents (i.e., a father and a son) or more like a relation that is internal to one agent (i.e., a man and his own wisdom)? The answer is both and neither. Given the Son's primacy, uniqueness, and transcendence, we must remember that, although there is a true family resemblance between the divine Son and creaturely sons, there is no one-to-one correspondence between the two. All analogies are partial. All analogies break down at some point.

How, then, are we to understand the Bible's distinctive uses of these analogies? What do they mean to teach us? While social analogies highlight the *real personal distinction* that exists between the first and second persons of the Trinity, psychological analogies highlight their *indivisible and inseparable oneness*. Put in theological idiom, while the persons of the Father and the Son are truly distinct, their distinction does not constitute a division in God's simple being. Unlike matters on the human plane, where the multiplication of human *persons* amounts to a multiplication of human *beings*, the multiplication of persons in God does not amount to a multiplication of gods. Scripture presents, and we praise, *one* God in *three* persons: the Father, the Son, and the Holy Spirit.

This is why the confession that the Son is "begotten, not made" goes hand in hand with the confession that the Son is "consubstantial with the Father." Except for the personal property by which he is distinguished from the Father (i.e., filiation), the only begotten Son is one with the Father in every respect. The Son is one God with the Father in his being, attributes, works, and worship. The Son is the Lord our God (John 20:28; 1 Cor. 8:6). He is one (1 Cor. 8:6), self-existent (John 5:26), immutable (Heb. 1:12; 13:8), and eternal (John 8:58). He is the wisdom of God and the power of God (1 Cor. 1:24), and the fullness of divine grace and truth (John 1:14). The Son is the Creator and preserver of all things (John 1:3; Col. 1:16–17; Heb. 1:2–3), the Redeemer and ruler of God's people (Eph. 1:3–23; Heb. 1:3–4; Rev. 1:5–6), the alpha and the omega, the first and the last, the beginning and the end (Rev. 22:13). To him alone, who is one God with the Father, worship is due (Phil. 2:9–11; Rev. 5:6–14; 22:9).

In confessing that the Son is "begotten, not made, consubstantial with the Father," the church preserves the personal distinction between the Father and the Son without dividing God's simple being. In this way, Christians honor the Son just as they honor the Father (John 5:23). This way of honoring the Son, however, is not undisputed. In the section that follows, we will consider three alternative ways of describing the Son that misidentify him and thereby dishonor him.

Misidentifying the Son

In everyday life, cases of mistaken identity come in various sorts. One thinks his wife is calling him from another room, but it turns out to be his daughter. One believes a person was born in Winston-Salem, North Carolina, when in fact she was born in St. Louis, Missouri. As these examples suggest, cases of mistaken identity can be relatively minor. But cases of mistaken identity can also be major, as when the wrong person is convicted of a crime. The same goes for cases of mistaken identity in theology. In this life, we know in part (1 Cor. 13:9, 12) and we err in many ways (James 3:2), including ways unknown to us (Ps. 19:12). Nevertheless, while some theological errors are relatively minor, others are very serious, indeed, potentially damning. For this reason, Paul strictly warns the church against false Christs and false gospels (2 Cor. 11:4; Gal. 1:6–9).

In the remaining section of this chapter, we will consider three serious cases of mistaken identity regarding the second person of the Trinity: modalism, subordinationism, and eternal functional subordinationism. The first two errors are classical Trinitarian heresies that were refuted by the church in the third and fourth centuries but have reappeared in various forms throughout the history of the church. The third error, of more recent provenance, does not exhibit the same degree of error or impiety as the first two. Nevertheless, it is a serious error that Christians should roundly reject because it inaccurately represents biblical teaching on the Trinity and therefore fails to provide a solid foundation for faith in the Trinity. Though these three examples do not constitute an exhaustive catalog of errors pertaining to the second person of the Trinity, they are, as far as Trinitarian errors go, representative, pervasive, and influential. They therefore warrant our attention.

The first error, modalism, affirms the oneness of God's being but denies the real, eternal distinction of the divine persons. According to modalism, the three persons of the Trinity have no real and distinct existence apart from God's interaction with the world. The three persons are merely different modes of God's interaction with the world, divine emanations that come into existence to accomplish God's work in the world and then cease to exist when God's work in the world is completed. Because it does not observe any real distinctions between the Father and the Son, modalism can speak as easily of the Father dying on the cross (the error known as patripassianism) as it can speak of the Son dying on the cross. Modalism, thus described, is an attack on Jesus's *personal dignity*: his eternal distinction from the Father and the Spirit, his existence before the creation of the world, his distinctive office of Mediator, and his continuing existence as an object of worship in the eternal kingdom of God. Various forms of modalism have been proposed by thinkers such as Sabellius in the third century, Marcellus of Ancyra in the fourth century, and Oneness Pentecostals today.

The second error, subordinationism, affirms a real distinction between the persons of the Trinity but denies that the second and third persons are one God with the first person of the Trinity. Subordinationism, in some of its forms, represents a response to modalism's failure to distinguish the persons of the Trinity. However, the cure it proposes is as bad as, if not worse than, the disease it seeks to treat. Subordinationism views the distinction between the Father, who begets, and the Son, who is begotten, as a distinction between a divine producer and a creaturely product, not as a distinction between divine persons. To beget, in this scheme, is to be divine. To be begotten, in this scheme, is to be a creature. Subordinationism can sometimes ascribe deity to the Son, but it is a diminished form of deity, not the selfsame, simple deity of God the Father. The Son, on subordinationism's terms, is a lesser deity, a created deity, who functions as a quasi-mediator between the one true God, the Father, and the rest of his creatures. For subordinationism, our redeemer is a creature, albeit God's most eminent creature, but one who, nevertheless, is not worthy of the same worship due to God the Father. Subordinationism, thus described, is an attack on Jesus's *true deity*: his eternal, consubstantial deity with the Father, his status as our divine Redeemer and Lord, his worthiness, with the Father, to receive supreme honor and glory. Early forms of subordinationism were proposed by thinkers such as Arius and Eunomius in the fourth century. Subordinationism witnessed a significant revival in the sixteenth century under the influence of various anti-Trinitarians, and still exists today in both scholarly and popular forms (e.g., Jehovah's Witnesses).

Before we proceed to the third error, it is worth pausing to assess the first two. The first two errors, especially in their third- and fourth-century manifestations, exhibit a number of common problems. Most fundamentally, they exhibit a failure to take into account the whole counsel of God with respect to the person of the Son. Subordinationism especially clings to scriptural texts that speak of the Son's incarnate nature, activity, and suffering, ignoring those texts that speak of his divine identity and dignity. These errors also exhibit a failure to appreciate the analogical character of scriptural revelation, often trying to make sense of biblical teaching about the Son's person, perfection, and work by means of univocal categories. They fail, in other words, to honor the Son's primacy, uniqueness, and transcendence.

The result of the first two errors is not only a diminished view of the person of the Son in particular but also a diminished view of God more generally. Because they fail to acknowledge the Father's eternal begetting of the Son and their mutual, eternal breathing forth of the Spirit, both modalism and subordinationism are unable to affirm that God is eternally, internally fruitful and productive in and of himself. For both views, fruitfulness and productivity are true of God not in and of himself but only insofar as he is Creator and Redeemer. In sum, modalism and subordinationism affirm unbiblical, impoverished views of God.

The third error, eternal functional subordinationism (hereafter EFS)—also known as eternal relations of authority and submission (hereafter ERAS)—is of more recent vintage. Its major proponents include conservative evangelical Protestants such as Wayne Grudem, Bruce Ware, and Owen Strachan. Though EFS affirms the eternal distinction of the persons of the Trinity, and though it affirms their full deity, both affirmations are compromised by the significant revisions it makes to classical Christian teaching on the Trinity. Rather than distinguishing the persons of the Trinity by means of relations of origin (i.e., paternity, filiation, and spiration), ERAS distinguishes the persons by means of relations of authority and submission.[4] The personal property of the Father lies in his eternal authority over the Son and the Spirit. The personal property of the Son lies in his eternal submission to the Father and his eternal authority over the Spirit. The personal property of the Spirit lies in his eternal submission to the Father and the Son.

This revision to classical Christian teaching regarding the personal properties of the Trinity brings with it further revisions to classical Christian teaching regarding the nature of God. Rather than recognizing divine authority and divine willing as common properties of the three persons, ERAS treats these attributes as personal properties, dividing them among

---

4. Though relations of origin have not played a significant role in the development of ERAS teaching on the Trinity over the past several decades, recently both Wayne Grudem and Bruce Ware have publicly affirmed their commitment to the doctrine of the eternal generation of the Son. This affirmation has not entailed the rejection of eternal relations of authority and submission, however. Ware's most recent summary of his views on the doctrine of the Trinity may be found in Bruce A. Ware, "Unity and Distinction of the Trinitarian Persons," in *Trinitarian Theology: Theological Models and Doctrinal Application*, ed. Keith S. Whitfield (Nashville: B&H Academic, 2017).

the three persons. The Father has an authority in relation to the Son that the Son lacks, and so forth. Moreover, ERAS seems to affirm that each person possesses his own distinct will, with the Father commanding the Son, the Son obeying the Father, the Father and the Son commanding the Spirit, and the Spirit obeying the Father and the Son. In turning common properties into personal properties, ERAS thus effectively denies divine simplicity as well.

ERAS has been the source of not a little controversy among Reformed and evangelical Christians in recent years, and not without reason. Although a spectrum of views falls under the heading of ERAS, reflecting varying degrees of error and impiety, many of its most basic tenets are quite problematic, and its most extreme expression exhibits a number of grave theological errors.[5] Classical Christian teaching on the Trinity set important boundary lines in distinguishing the divine persons by means of relations of origin and in preserving their divine oneness by means of divine simplicity. Because these boundary lines accord with the canons of biblical reasoning, they cannot be transgressed without serious consequences. Despite ERAS's laudable commitment to biblical authority, a less laudable com-

---

5. Bruce Ware's book *Father, Son, and Holy Spirit: Relationships, Roles, Relevance* (Wheaton, IL: Crossway, 2005) is a mixture of legitimate theological summary, questionable or odd expressions, and serious error. Particularly disastrous, in my judgment, is the manner in which the book spells out the relations of authority and submission, both within the Trinity and outside the Trinity in God's external works. For example, in speaking of relations internal to the Trinity, the Father is described as "supreme over" all things, including the Son and the Spirit (pp. 46ff.). "The Father stands above the Son" (p. 49), "has supremacy over the Son" (p. 50), receives "the ultimate glory" (p. 50) over the Son, whose glory is "penultimate" in relation to the Father (p. 154). The Father is "supreme within the Godhead as the highest authority and the one deserving of ultimate praise" (p. 51). In speaking of the Trinity in its external works, the book denies the doctrine of inseparable operations and suggests that the Father exercises sovereignty over against the Son and the Spirit in determining whether or not he will act with and through them in his external works. Moreover, it suggests that, when the Father does choose to work through the Son and the Spirit, it is an act of grace and humility (pp. 57–58). I cannot find a charitable way of reading these statements as anything but significant transgressions of traditional Trinitarian orthodoxy. To its credit, Crossway no longer publishes the book.

mitment to biblicism as a theological method has led to a removal of ancient landmarks that should not be removed. While its affirmation of eternally distinct, fully divine persons retains an orthodox facade, its revision of personal properties and its division of God's simple being manifest profound structural instabilities.

In one way or another, then, each of the above approaches fails to honor the Son just as it honors the Father (John 5:23). Modalism denies the Son's personal dignity. Subordinationism denies the Son's true deity. Eternal functional subordinationism, though superficially affirming the Son's divine personhood and divine oneness with the Father, threatens to undermine both affirmations through its revision of personal properties and its division of God's simple being.

Conclusion

In Holy Scripture God presents Jesus Christ to us as his only begotten Son and our Lord, as our Creator and preserver, as our Redeemer and King. For this reason, the church, in receiving this Christ, confesses that he is "begotten, not made, consubstantial with the Father."

The church's confession in this regard is an act of obedience to God's self-revelation in Holy Scripture, not the solution to a metaphysical puzzle about unity and diversity, and certainly not an attempt to explain the tripersonal God's unfathomable being. The mystery of the Son's eternal begetting is one that mortal minds cannot fathom. Because it is a divine begetting, it is an unsearchable deep (Ps. 145:3; Rom. 11:33).

Nevertheless, because the mystery of the Son's eternal begetting is a revealed mystery, we can learn to follow the grammar of biblical discourse, we can learn to sing its tune, even if we cannot grasp the deeper laws of the music by which it operates.

Let us therefore acknowledge Jesus Christ as God's only begotten Son and our Lord, as our Creator and preserver, as our Redeemer and King. Let us receive him as such. And let us render to him, with hearts, lives, and lips, the worship that he alone, with the Father and the Spirit, deserves. For he is worthy (Rev. 5:9–14)!

6

God the Holy Spirit

With the Father and the Son, Christians praise the Holy Spirit; and for good reason. The Spirit of the Father (Matt. 10:20; Rom. 8:9) and the Son (Rom. 8:9; Gal. 4:6) is one God with the Father and the Son, the third person of the Trinity, and the crowning agent of God's undivided purpose and power (Eph. 4:4–6). Before all ages, the Spirit searched and shared the Father's sovereign purpose to glorify us in and through the Son for the sake of the Son (Isa. 40:13–14; Rom. 8:29; 1 Cor. 2:7–16). Because he is the fountain of life (Ps. 36:9), the Spirit gives life in the works of creation and providence (Gen. 1:2; Pss. 33:6; 104:27–30; 139). The Spirit indwelled and led the people of Israel in the exodus (Isa. 63:11–14; Hag. 2:5), empowered judges (Judg. 3:10), and anointed kings (1 Sam. 10:1, 6, 10). The Spirit announced Jesus's birth and caused him to be conceived in the virgin's womb (Luke 1:35, 41–42, 67–79). The Spirit alighted on Jesus at his baptism and empowered his public ministry by his anointing and abiding presence (Matt. 3:16–17; 12:28; Luke 10:21; John 1:33). "Through the eternal Spirit," Jesus offered himself to God as a redeeming sacrifice (Heb. 9:14–15).

"According to the Spirit of holiness," Jesus was appointed the Son of God with power by his resurrection from the dead (Rom. 1:4). On the occasion of his enthronement, Jesus poured out the Spirit as his coronation day blessing upon his people (John 7:39; Acts 2:33; Eph. 4:8). The Spirit consummates the triune work of salvation by communicating to us all the blessings purchased for us by the Son in his grace and purposed for us by the Father in his love (2 Cor. 13:14; Eph. 1:3).[1] Poured out upon us in our baptism through the proclamation of the word, the Spirit is operative in our regeneration, justification, adoption, and sanctification (John 3:3, 5; Acts 2:38; 1 Cor. 6:11; Gal. 4:6–7; Eph. 5:26; Titus 3:3–7). By his personal presence, he assures us of our glorification (Rom. 8:10, 15–17; Eph. 1:13–14) and grants us a foretaste of the all-satisfying, life-giving stream that flows from the throne of God and the Lamb in the eternal kingdom (1 Cor. 12:13; Rev. 22:1).

Thus, having considered the first and second persons of the Trinity in the preceding two chapters, we turn now to the third person of the Trinity. In considering patterns of scriptural naming related to the Holy Spirit, one is immediately struck by Scripture's relative lack of attention to the Spirit in comparison with the Father and the Son. As Gregory of Nazianzus observed long ago, this relative lack of attention is partially explained by the economy of Trinitarian revelation whereby the different persons of the Trinity are manifested with differing degrees of clarity at different phases of God's unfolding kingdom.[2] We witness a similar pattern in the development of the church's teaching on the Holy Spirit. The church began to clarify its

---

1. Petrus van Mastricht, *Theoretical-Practical Theology*, trans. Todd M. Rester, vol. 2 (Grand Rapids, MI: Reformation Heritage, 2019), 585–86.

2. Gregory of Nazianzus, *Oration* 31.26–27, in *On God and Christ: The Five Theological Orations and Two Letters to Cledonius* (Crestwood, NY: St Vladimir's Seminary Press, 2002), 137–38.

confession regarding the Holy Spirit only after it had clarified its confession regarding the Father and the Son.

But this explanation is not all there is to say. Another reason for Scripture's relative lack of attention to the Spirit in comparison to the Father and the Son has to do with the Spirit himself and the office he fulfills in God's unfolding kingdom. Jesus identifies the nature of the Holy Spirit's office in John 16:14: "He will glorify me." The Spirit who inspired prophets and apostles to announce God's word in Holy Scripture inspired them to focus on Jesus Christ: his person, his work, his promises (John 15:26–27; 1 Pet. 1:11). The Spirit's office in God's unfolding kingdom is to bear witness to Jesus Christ, holding him forth as God's beloved Son and our Lord, drawing us to embrace him, causing us to confess him as Lord, enabling us to take on our lips his own address of the Father (John 1:12–13; 1 Cor. 12:3; Gal. 4:6). Scripture, because it is inspired by the Spirit, bears the signature of the Spirit's office in its emphasis and end.

Far from being a bit role in the drama of God's unfolding kingdom, the Spirit's office manifests the distinctive glory of his person. As Jesus's baptism manifests in time his begetting in eternity, with the Father announcing and the Spirit anointing him as God's beloved Son, so Jesus's baptism manifests the Spirit's distinctive glory as the "crowning" person of the Trinity. When the Father declares, "You are my beloved Son," the Spirit descends as the divine seal of the Father's messianic declaration (Mark 1:9–11). In Jesus's baptism, the Father publicly crowns his only begotten Son, the Son is crowned, and the Spirit is the crown.

As the third person of the Trinity, the Spirit is the crowning procession in God's triune life *ad intra*, and the crowning agent of God's indivisible work *ad extra*. In the eternal procession of the Spirit from the Father and the Son, the perfect fruitfulness of God's triune life is fully realized. In the temporal mission of the

Spirit, the undivided work of the triune God in nature, grace, and glory is brought to consummation.

In what follows, we will first consider the scriptural grammar of naming with respect to the third person of the Trinity, focusing on Jesus's teaching about the Holy Spirit in John 16:12–15. We will then contemplate more deeply the mystery of his personal property—his "double procession" from the Father and the Son. As we will see, the Spirit who eternally proceeds in the mutual love of the Father and the Son, crowning God's triune life, comes in time to embrace God's people within God's triune life, thereby crowning God's external works to the glory of the triune God.

Naming God the Holy Spirit: The Basic Grammar

In his Farewell Discourse, with his looming departure in view, Jesus encourages his disciples by instructing them on a number of different topics. Central to his encouragement of the disciples is his teaching on the Holy Spirit. John 16:12–15 offers an excellent summary of that teaching that exhibits the basic grammar of scriptural naming with respect to the third person of the Trinity:

> I still have many things to say to you, but you cannot bear them now. When the Spirit of truth comes, he will guide you into all the truth, for he will not speak from himself, but whatever he hears he will speak, and he will declare to you the things that are to come. He will glorify me, for he will take what is mine and declare it to you. All that the Father has is mine; therefore I said that he will take what is mine and declare it to you. (ESV, altered)

In John 16:12–15, Jesus promises that the coming of the Holy Spirit will remedy the disciples' inability in that particular moment to bear all that Jesus desires to teach them. The disciples' inability is undoubtedly subjective in part. They do not have the subjective capacity to receive Jesus's teaching owing to their sorrow at his imminent departure, their spiritual immaturity, and so forth. But the disciples' inability to bear Jesus's teaching is not wholly subjective. Their inability is also due to their objective location within the unfolding events of redemptive history. Jesus has not yet died, he has not yet risen, and he has not yet ascended to the right hand of the Father. The disciples cannot possibly understand and appreciate the full significance of those events before they take place. Until they occur, their meaning and significance must remain a riddle (John 16:25).

According to Jesus, "the Spirit of truth" will remedy the disciples' situation by guiding them "into all the truth" (John 16:13). As the broader context of the Farewell Discourse indicates, guiding the disciples into all the truth includes causing them to remember all the things that Jesus has already taught them (John 14:26). As the present context indicates, guiding the disciples into all the truth also involves declaring to them "the things that are to come" (John 16:13). In sum, when the Spirit comes, he will enable the disciples to remember, grasp, and faithfully bear witness to all that Jesus has taught them and all that Jesus has yet to teach them (John 15:26–27; 20:21–23). The Gospel of John itself is a literary testament to the Spirit's fulfillment of Jesus's promise.

In John 16:14, Jesus further explains that the Spirit's work of guiding the disciples into all the truth has a reference not only to Jesus as teacher (i.e., what he has taught, what he has yet to teach) but also to Jesus as subject matter: "He will glorify me." What Jesus has been teaching the disciples, what he longs yet to teach them, and what the Spirit will do in fulfilling

Jesus's pedagogical intention all revolve around Jesus's person and glory. This is what Jesus came to teach the disciples. This is what the disciples, and those who will hear their testimony, need to know: the glory of Jesus Christ. They need to know the glory he had with the Father before the foundation of the world (John 17:24), the glory he manifested in his incarnation (John 1:14), and the glory he will manifest in his crucifixion, resurrection, ascension, and enthronement at the Father's right hand (John 7:39; 12:27–28). This further confirms a point made at the outset of this chapter: the distinctive office of the Holy Spirit in God's unfolding kingdom is to glorify Jesus Christ, God's only begotten Son. God the Spirit crowns God the Son by causing the glory of his eternal, incarnate, crucified, and exalted person to be proclaimed, received, and celebrated to the glory of God the Father (John 20:20; 1 John 1:4).

What qualifies the Spirit for this office? Jesus offers three qualifications, each of which illumines the Spirit's distinct identity as the third person of the Trinity. The Spirit is qualified to lead the disciples into all the truth concerning the glory of Jesus Christ because, says Jesus, (1) he is "the Spirit of truth" (John 16:13), (2) "he will not speak from himself, but whatever he hears he will speak" (John 16:13), and (3) "he will take what is mine and declare it to you" (John 16:14). The first qualification, the Spirit's title as "the Spirit of truth," identifies the Spirit by means of his relation to Jesus. Jesus has already identified himself as "the truth" (John 14:6). Here he identifies the Spirit as "the Spirit of truth." The second qualification, the fact that the Spirit will speak not "from himself" but only what "he hears," again identifies the Spirit by means of his relation to someone else. In this case, the Spirit does not speak from himself, but he speaks what he hears from someone else. The third qualification clarifies from whom the Spirit speaks: "He will take what is mine and declare it to you. All that the Father has is mine; therefore I said that he will take what is mine and declare it to you" (John 16:14–15). The Spirit speaks from the Son, taking what the Son holds in common with the Father and declaring it to the disciples.

With this overview in place, it is time to take stock of what John 16:12–15 teaches us about the third person of the Trinity. Note, first, that, according to this text, the Spirit is no ordinary emissary. The Spirit holds all things in common with the Father and the Son. All that the Father has belongs to the Son. All that the Son has belongs to the Spirit (vv. 14–15). And here "all" means all. The Spirit is able to glorify the Son because he has access to all of the Son's glory—the glory he received from the Father before the foundation of the world, the glory of the Father and Son's common purpose for the world, and the glory of the Father and Son's undivided work in the world. Because the Spirit possesses all things in the infinite treasury of God's being, the Spirit is able to share all things with God's people, indeed to fill them up "with all the fullness of God" (Eph. 3:19). In theological idiom, because the Spirit is consubstantial with the Father and the Son, he is an agent of their undivided agency.

Note, second, how John 16:12–15 describes the Spirit's personal distinction from the Father and the Son. That personal distinction does not lie in *what* the Spirit has. As we observed in the preceding point, the Spirit has all things in common with the Father and the Son. The Spirit's personal distinction from the other two persons lies in the *way* he has what he has.[3] In both his personal mode of existence and his personal mode of acting, the Spirit is and acts from the Father and the Son. What he has, he "takes" from the Father and the Son (vv. 14–15). What he

3. Thomas Aquinas, *Commentary on the Gospel of John, Chapters 13–21*, trans. Fabian Larcher (Washington, DC: Catholic University of America Press, 2010), 145.

speaks, he does not speak "from himself" (v. 13). As "the Spirit of truth," he speaks "whatever he hears" from the Father and the Son (v. 13). Again, his distinction from the Father and the Son lies not in what he has—"the truth"—but in the way he has what he has—as "the Spirit of truth"—a point we will explore more fully in the next section.

Note, third, that John 16:12–18 teaches us something important about what it means for the Spirit to be a divine person. The Greek term for "Spirit" used throughout our text is neuter. However, Jesus refers to the Spirit throughout our text by means of masculine pronouns. The Spirit, according to Jesus, is "he" not "it." Moreover, Jesus describes the Spirit as one who "comes," "guides," "hears," "speaks," "declares," "glorifies," and "takes." In each instance, the verb indicates the action of a personal agent, not the movement of an inanimate object or force, a "who" not a "what."

What does this teach us about what it means for the Spirit to be a divine person? Not only must we affirm that the Spirit is an eternal, distinct, existing relation within the Trinity, in keeping with the lessons we have learned already (and guarding against modalism). But according to John 16:12–15, we must also affirm that the Spirit is an eternal, distinct, existing relation *of a certain kind*. That is to say, the Spirit is an eternal, distinct, existing relation who is capable of coming, guiding, hearing, speaking, declaring, glorifying, and taking. What is true of the Spirit in this regard is true of the Father and the Son as well. According to classical Christian teaching, a divine person is an eternal, distinct, existing relation of a "rational nature."[4]

It is interesting to observe that, as is the case in the person of the Son, so too in the person of the Spirit, Scripture uses both

---

4. Boethius defines a person as "the individual substance of a rational nature" (*A Treatise against Eutyches and Nestorius*, Loeb Classical Library 74 [Cambridge: Harvard University Press, 1973], 3.4–5).

"social" and "psychological" analogies to reveal the character of his divine personhood. In texts like John 16:12–15, Scripture uses social analogies, portraying the Spirit as a distinct speech agent who hears and speaks in relation to other distinct speech agents, preeminently the Father and the Son. In other places, Scripture uses psychological analogies, portraying the Spirit as God's "breath," who bears the "Word" God utters in calling creation into existence (e.g., Ps. 33:6), and as the Spirit/mind within God that searches God's own inner thoughts (e.g., 1 Cor. 2:11). While the former analogies preserve the real distinction between the Spirit and the other persons of the Trinity, the latter analogies preserve the simple oneness of God by portraying the procession of the Spirit as internal to God's being.

Naming God the Spirit: Digging Deeper

It is time to explore more deeply what it means for the Spirit to proceed from the Father and the Son. We begin with Jesus's statement in John 16:13: "He will not speak from himself, but whatever he hears he will speak" (ESV, altered). As we saw in the preceding section, the Spirit's *speaking* to the disciples, his office of guiding them into all the truth concerning Jesus, is rooted in his *hearing*. His work in relation to the disciples is rooted in his relation to someone else. Moreover, the comprehensive nature of his speaking is rooted in the comprehensive nature of his hearing. The Spirit is qualified to lead the disciples "into all the truth" concerning Jesus (John 16:13) because he hears "all" the truth concerning Jesus, all that Jesus holds in common with the Father (John 16:15). The question we must explore more fully now is this: Whence the Spirit's hearing and speaking?

The answer, according to the Gospel of John, as well as the rest of Holy Scripture, is that the Spirit hears and speaks not from himself but from the Father and the Son. The third person of the Trinity is the Spirit who "hears" the words of the Father concerning the Son and the words of the Son concerning the Father, contemplating the eternal divine depths of the word that the Father utters and the Word that the Son is (1 Cor. 2:10–11). The third person of the Trinity is the divine "breath" that bears those words from the speaking Father to the hearing Son, and from the speaking Son to the hearing Father. In turn, the third person of the Trinity "speaks" those words to the prophets and apostles and, through them, to us in the God-breathed Scriptures (John 15:26–27; 20:21–23; 1 Cor. 2:12–13; 2 Tim. 3:16), "what the Spirit says to the churches" (Rev. 2:7).

In Johannine idiom, the Spirit hears the glory given by the Father to the Son before the foundation of the world, the glory given because the Father loved the Son before the foundation of the world (John 17:24). The Spirit hears the Father's eternal utterance to the Son:

> You are my Son;
> > today I have begotten you. (Ps. 2:7; see also John 1:1)

The Spirit hears the Father's eternal appointment of the Son to be the Redeemer, Lord, and heir of all things:

> Ask of me, and I will make the nations your heritage,
> > and the ends of the earth your possession. (Ps. 2:8; see
> > > also Heb. 1:2)

The Spirit hears the Father speak the world into existence through the Son (Gen. 1:1–3; John 1:3). The Spirit hears the Father declare his pleasure in the Son at his baptism and transfiguration (Mark 1:11; 9:7). The Spirit hears the Father install the Son as Priest and King at the Father's right hand (Ps. 110:1; Mark 12:35–37). The Spirit hears all things, in eternity and time, that the Father utters concerning the Son. And this is what qualifies the Spirit to reveal all things concerning the Son, in eternity and time, to us. As the comprehensive auditor of the glory given by the Father to the Son, the Spirit is the comprehensive revealer of the glory given by the Father to the Son (John 16:14).

The converse is true as well. The Word eternally uttered by God is a Word who faces God, addressing God (John 1:1). The divine Word has "many things to say" (John 16:12), and the Spirit "hears" and "speak[s]" them all (John 16:13). In Proverbs 8:22–31, the second person of the Trinity, speaking under the persona of divine Wisdom, tells of his relationship to the first person of the Trinity before and in the creation of the world. According to Proverbs 1:23, divine Wisdom makes his words known to us by his Spirit:

> If you turn at my reproof,
> behold, I will pour out my spirit to you;
>> I will make my words known to you.

In similar fashion, the words spoken by the Father to the Son in Psalm 2:7 ("You are my Son; / today I have begotten you") are in fact reported to us by the Son ("I will tell of the decree: / The LORD said to me . . ."). And these intratrinitarian words, in turn, come to us because David speaks "in the Holy Spirit" (Mark 12:36).

Again, to borrow Johannine idiom, the Spirit does not hear or speak "from himself" (John 16:13); he hears and speaks from the Father and the Son, and he "take[s]" from them and "glorif[ies]" them (John 16:14–15). This pattern reveals the distinctive character of the Spirit's personhood, that which distinguishes the third person of the Trinity from the first and second persons. As the Father's distinct personal mode of existing is to exist from no one but to beget the Son and breathe the Spirit, and as the Son's distinct personal mode of existing is to be begotten of the Father and to breathe the Spirit, so the Spirit's distinct personal mode of existing is to proceed from the Father and the Son. Furthermore, as the Father's distinct personal mode of acting is to act from no one but to act through the Son and by the Spirit, and as the Son's distinct personal mode of acting is to act from the Father by the Spirit, so the Spirit's personal mode of acting is to act from the Father and the Son. The Spirit's "procession," the manner in which he is "breathed forth," is double. The Spirit proceeds from the Father and the Son in eternity, and he comes to us from the Father and the Son in time.

The pattern we have observed here is confirmed in a wide variety of ways throughout Scripture. The Spirit is named the Spirit of the Father (Matt. 10:20) and the Spirit of the Son (Gal. 4:6). He is called the Spirit of God and the Spirit of Christ (Rom. 8:9). The Spirit who proceeds from the Father (John 15:26) is also breathed forth by the Son (John 20:22). As one who proceeds from the Father and the Son, the Spirit is sent by the Father (John 14:16, 26) and the Son (John 15:26; 16:7) to God's people. The Father sends the Spirit in Jesus's name (John 14:26). The Son sends the Spirit from the Father (John 15:26). In all of these ways and many others, the Spirit's distinctive personal identity and agency are indicated by means of the Spirit's double relation of origin. He is the Spirit of the Father and the Son.

The double procession of the Spirit lies at the heart of the greatest schism in the Christian church, with churches in the West affirming the Spirit's double procession and churches in the East disputing it.[5] Space forbids addressing this very com-

---

5. For further discussion, see A. Edward Siecienski, *The Filioque: History of a Doctrinal Controversy* (Oxford: Oxford University Press, 2010).

plex debate at any length. However, a few brief comments are in order.

Reformed theologians have often expressed sympathy for the Eastern church's complaint about the Western church's addition of the so-called Filioque clause to the Nicene-Constantinopolitan Creed.[6] Reformed theologians have also wanted to affirm the doctrinal truth of the Filioque because they are convinced (for reasons such as those outlined above) that it is the teaching of Holy Scripture. Furthermore, they have looked for ways of bridging the theological, if not the creedal, divide between Eastern and Western churches by noting that, according to its mature Augustinian expression, the double procession of the Spirit comes about from a single principle that lies in the Father,[7] and that, according to certain Eastern formulations, the Spirit's single procession comes about from the Father "through" the Son. However close these statements may or may not be, the Reformed do not believe these doctrinal differences warrant ecclesiastical division.[8]

The doctrine of the Spirit's double procession from the Father and the Son has in its favor not only the scriptural arguments outlined above. The doctrine also clarifies the distinction between the second and third persons of the Trinity. Fundamental to the difference between the second and third persons is the fact that the former has a single relation of origin (he is eternally begotten of the Father), whereas the latter has a twofold relation of origin (he eternally proceeds from the Father and the Son). If relations of origin are what fundamentally distinguish

---

6. That is, the clause which states that the Spirit "proceeds from the Father *and the Son.*"

7. The argument is that, because the Son personally receives everything he has from the Father, this must include the property of breathing forth the Spirit as well. Thus, while the Spirit proceeds from the Father and the Son, he does so from one "spirating" principle, which resides originally in the Father and, by virtue of eternal begetting, also in the Son.

8. Van Mastricht, *Theoretical-Practical Theology*, 2:582–84.

the persons of the Trinity from each other, then losing that which distinguishes the second and third persons from each other would be an enormous loss for theological understanding.

Furthermore, the doctrine of the Spirit's double procession from the Father and the Son has in its favor a practical benefit. The procession of the Spirit from the Son reminds us that the Spirit does not exist or act independently of the Son, but the Spirit exists and acts from the Word and for the Word. He comes from Jesus Christ to glorify Jesus Christ (John 16:7, 14). Consequently, all true "spirituality," all Trinitarian spirituality, will seek the power of the Spirit of Christ and will devote itself to the glory of Christ. And it will pursue both in accordance with the ways we are instructed to pursue them in Holy Scripture, the Spirit's inspired witness to Jesus Christ. To seek any other spirit or to devote oneself to any other spiritual end is not to follow the Holy Spirit but to follow the spirit of antichrist (1 John 4:1–3).

Conclusion

I began this chapter by affirming the Christian praise of God the Holy Spirit. And rightly so: the Holy Spirit is the third person of the holy Trinity, one God with the Father and the Son in his being, attributes, works, and worship. In the Spirit's name we baptize (Matt. 28:19); in his name we bless (2 Cor. 13:14); against his name we are warned not to blaspheme (Matt. 12:31–32). We conclude this chapter with the observation, made by Petrus van Mastricht, that the Spirit is not only the object of Christian praise. The Spirit is also the cause of Christian praise, the one who opens before our eyes and causes us to enter the kingdom of praise to our triune King (John 3:3, 5; Rev. 4–5).[9]

The Holy Spirit is the cause of Christian praise because he is the crowning procession of the holy Trinity. In the Spirit, the Fa-

---

9. Van Mastricht, *Theoretical-Practical Theology*, 2:581–82.

ther crowns the Son as Lord: first in eternity (John 17:24–26), then in history (Rom. 1:4), then in our hearts (1 Cor. 12:3). As the one who shares the Father's purpose and empowers the Son's work, the Spirit brings it about that we come to acknowledge, receive, and rejoice in the good things that the Father has accomplished and announced in his beloved Son, our Lord Jesus Christ.

And so it is fitting to conclude this chapter with a prayer that, by his Spirit, the Father would crown Jesus as Lord in our hearts:

> For this reason I bow my knees before the Father, from whom every family in heaven and on earth is named, that according to the riches of his glory he may grant you to be strengthened with power through his Spirit in your inner being, so that Christ may dwell in your hearts through faith—that you, being rooted and grounded in love, may have strength to comprehend with all the saints what is the breadth and length and height and depth, and to know the love of Christ that surpasses knowledge, that you may be filled with all the fullness of God.
>
> Now to him who is able to do far more abundantly than all we ask or think, according to the power at work within us, to him be glory in the church and in Christ Jesus throughout all generations, forever and ever. Amen. (Eph. 3:14–21)

7

The Shape of God's Triune Work

Christians praise the triune God for his being and works, following on earth the pattern of the liturgy performed in heaven. The heavenly hosts acclaim the perfect holiness of the Lord God Almighty and acknowledge the eternal and unchanging majesty of his transcendent being:

> Holy, holy, holy, is the Lord God Almighty,
>> who was and is and is to come! (Rev. 4:8)

They also glorify God for his works of creation, preservation, redemption, and consummation. They praise God the Creator and preserver of all things:

> Worthy are you, our Lord and God,
>> to receive glory and honor and power,
> for you created all things,
>> and by your will they existed and were created.
>> (Rev. 4:11)

They praise God the Redeemer of his people:

> Worthy are you to take the scroll
>   and to open its seals,
> for you were slain, and by your blood you ransomed
>   people for God
>   from every tribe and language and people and nation,
> and you have made them a kingdom and priests to our
>   God. (Rev. 5:9–10)

They praise God the consummator, who will one day bring to completion his works of creation and redemption: "and they shall reign on the earth" (Rev. 5:10). The perfect praise of heaven, acknowledging the worthiness of God in his being and works, is offered "in the Spirit" (Rev. 4:2), the cause of divine worship (Rev. 4:5; 5:6), "To him who sits on the throne and to the Lamb" (Rev. 5:13).

In praising God's works, Christian theology distinguishes between actions that remain within God, his "internal operations," and actions whose effects occur outside of God, his "external operations." Actions that remain within God include those that account for God's triunity itself—that is, the Father's eternal begetting of the Son, and the Father and Son's eternal breathing forth of the Spirit. God's internal operations also include his eternal plan and purpose for creatures, his eternal decree. Actions whose effects occur outside of God—actions properly described as God's "works"—include the works of creation, providence, redemption, sanctification, and consummation. God's internal operations have no beginning or end. They are eternal, fully actualized realities. They are what constitute God the eternally lively, eternally tripersonal God that he is. God's external operations, though having an eternal root within God's eternal plan and purpose for creatures, are different. All created effects of God have a beginning and an end. They progress, they develop, they change. They live and die; and some of them live again.

God's external works manifest the splendor of his being, attributes, and persons in myriad ways. God's external works are guided by his wisdom, expressive of his goodness, performed by his power, and aimed at his glory. "From him and through him and to him are all things. To him be glory forever. Amen" (Rom. 11:36). God's external works exhibit a Trinitarian shape, proceeding from the Father, through the Son, in the Spirit; and God's external works exhibit a Trinitarian stamp, whether more faint, as in the products of his creative work, or more pronounced, as in the products of his redeeming and consummating works.

In previous chapters, I have focused on God's internal operations, the acts that constitute God the eternally lively, eternally tripersonal God that he is. In the present chapter, I will focus on God's external operations. More specifically, we will examine the shape of God's tripersonal agency and the stamp it impresses on its creaturely effects. Our discussion will proceed as follows: First, we will consider the general shape of God's triune work. Then, we will consider two specific applications of God's triune work, Trinitarian "appropriations" and Trinitarian "missions."

One God, Three Persons in Action

As we have seen in earlier chapters, God's primacy, uniqueness, and transcendence teach us that we should not think of God's triune being in a creaturely way. While creatures bear a family resemblance to God—he is the Father from whom every family in heaven and on earth is named (Eph. 3:14–15)—there is no one-to-one correspondence between God and creatures; he is the Father of lights with whom there is no variation or shadow due to change (James 1:17). As we have also seen, God's primacy, uniqueness, and transcendence teach us something about the way he uses creaturely language to reveal himself to us. When God speaks to creatures by means of creaturely language, he puts that language to new and different uses. God calls himself "Father" and "Son." And these names indicate something profound and true about God, including the real distinction that exists between the first and second persons of the Trinity. But the distinction between the first and second persons is not like the distinction between a human father and a human son. Two human persons makes two human beings. Not so with God. Thus God also calls himself "God" and "Word," indicating that the distinction between the first and second persons of the Trinity is not a distinction between two divine beings—two gods—but a distinction within the one being of the one God.

What is true of God's being is true of God's action as well. The works of God are not a matter of three friends getting together, each doing his part, to accomplish a common goal. Nor are the works of God the exhibition of an indistinct force. The works of God are the works of the thrice-holy Trinity. As such, God's works bear the marks of God's primacy, uniqueness, and transcendence. God's agency is first in the order of acting; indeed, it is the beginning and end of all other agencies (Rom. 11:36; Rev. 1:17). God's agency is unique. Not belonging to a class with other agents, God's agency is "over all and through all and in all" (Eph. 4:6). God's agency is transcendent, not contained or constrained by creaturely space and time, height or depth, strength or weakness (1 Kings 8:27–30; Ps. 139:7–16; 1 Cor. 1:25; Rev. 4:8).

Consequently, when Scripture speaks of divine agency, it employs both social and psychological analogies to reveal something of God's majestic and incomparable agency. Scripture portrays God as a sovereign King who speaks the world into existence by his sovereign Word and Spirit (Ps. 33:6). Scripture portrays God as a father who sends a beloved son on a mission to gather the fruits of his vineyard (Mark 12:1–12). And as these analogies teach us something about God's triune being, so they teach us something about his triune action. What is that lesson? As God's being is simple and indivisible, so his works are undivided and inseparable. As three distinct persons eternally exist within God's simple, indivisible being, so there is a threefold order of operation within God's undivided, inseparable works.

All of God's external works are indivisible works of the one God: guided by God's singular divine wisdom, expressive of God's singular divine goodness, performed by God's singular divine power, aimed at God's singular divine glory. Moreover, because the one God is three persons, the mutual relations between the persons of the Trinity exhibit themselves within God's indivisible external works. As the Father's distinct personal mode of existing is to exist from no one but to beget the Son and breathe the Spirit, so the Father's distinct personal mode of acting is to act from no one but to act through the Son and by the Spirit. As the Son's distinct personal mode of existing is to exist from the Father as his only begotten and to breathe the Spirit, so the Son's distinct personal mode of acting is to act from the Father and by the Spirit. As the Spirit's distinct personal mode of existing is to be eternally breathed forth by the Father and the Son as the crowning procession of the Trinity, so his distinctive personal mode of acting is to act from the Father and the Son, bringing all of God's undivided external operations to their crowning fulfillment. The one God's distinct personal modes of existing as Father, Son, and Spirit are inflected in the Trinitarian shape of God's indivisible action: God's external actions proceed from the Father, through the Son, in the Spirit.

In the next two sections, we will consider two specific applications of the Trinitarian shape of God's undivided actions: appropriations and missions. Both applications provide deeper insight into the wonder of God's triune work.

Appropriations

Let us review the ground we have covered. Because God is one, all God's actions with respect to creatures are indivisible actions of all three persons of the Trinity. The internal operation of the divine decree is an indivisible operation performed by all three persons (John 15:16; 1 Cor. 2:7–11; Eph. 1:4–5), as are the external operations of creation (Gen. 1:1–3; Ps. 33:6), redemption (Gal. 4:4–7), and consummation (Rev. 22:1–5). Because God is three, all of God's actions with respect to creatures manifest a Trinitarian shape, proceeding from the Father through the Son in the Spirit. Because he is the first person of the Trinity, from whom the other persons proceed, the Father initiates God's indivisible operations. Because he is the second person of the Trinity, begotten of the Father, the Son accomplishes God's indivisible operations. Because he is the third person of the Trinity, proceeding from the Father and the Son, the Spirit brings God's indivisible operations to their crowning effects. This Trinitarian shape is evident in the work of creation, where the Father speaks, the Son is the Father's Word, and the Spirit is the breath that bears the Father's divine utterance in the Son and causes the things that the Father has spoken into being through the Son to be what God has called them to be (Gen. 1:1–3; Ps. 33:6; John 1:3). This Trinitarian shape is also evident in the work of redemption, where the Father sends the Son to redeem, the

Son comes from the Father to accomplish redemption, and the Spirit comes from the Father and the Son to apply redemption (Gal. 4:4–7).

All of God's works with respect to creatures are common to all three persons of the Trinity. All of God's works with respect to creatures follow a Trinitarian shape: proceeding from the Father through the Son in the Spirit. That said, certain divine works are often specially associated with certain persons of the Trinity. For example, Scripture specially identifies the Father as the author of the divine decree (Eph. 1:4–5) and as the agent of creation (Eph. 3:9; James 1:17; Rev. 4:11). Scripture specially identifies the Son as the agent of redemption (2 Cor. 8:9; Eph. 1:7; Rev. 5:9–10). Scripture specially identifies the Spirit as the agent of sanctification—that is, the one who dwells within us, applies the effects of God's redeeming work to us, and causes us to call upon God's name (1 Cor. 12:3; Gal. 4:6; Eph. 1:13).

Why is this the case? The answer is not because the Father alone decrees and creates or because the Son alone redeems or because the Spirit alone sanctifies. All of these works are common to all three persons of the Trinity. All of these works are undivided operations of the three persons. Here is where Christian teaching about Trinitarian "appropriations" comes into play.

Scripture specially identifies distinct persons of the Trinity with distinct works of the Trinity because certain works more specially manifest certain persons of the Trinity. Thus, as the Father is the first person of the Trinity, the personal fountain from whom the other persons of the Trinity proceed, Scripture appropriates the internal operation of the decree to the Father because the decree is the fountain from which all of God's external operations flow (Rom. 11:33). Likewise, Scripture appropriates the external operation of creation to the Father, the first person of the Trinity, because creation is the first of God's external operations, and because creation involves a kind of "fathering" of all creatures (Ps. 90:2; James 1:17). In similar fashion, as the Son is the second person of the Trinity, who is begotten of the Father and breathes the Spirit, Scripture appropriates the work of redemption to the Son because redemption is the second of God's external operations, and because redemption involves the making of "sons" out of slaves (John 1:12; Gal. 4:5–6). In similar fashion, as the Spirit is the third person of the Trinity, who proceeds from the Father and the Son, Scripture appropriates the work of sanctification to the Holy Spirit because sanctification is the third of God's external operations, and because sanctification involves making us both holy (1 Pet. 1:2) and alive (John 3:6; 6:63; 7:37–39).

Triadic patterns of appropriating specific works of the Trinity to specific persons of the Trinity are evident in texts such as Ephesians 1:3–14 and Revelation 4–5, revealing a deep Trinitarian logic at work in scriptural discourse concerning God. Triadic patterns of appropriation are also exhibited in three-article creeds like the Apostles' Creed, which appropriates creation to the Father, redemption to the Son, and sanctification to the Spirit.[1] Learning to follow scriptural patterns of appropriation is thus essential to Christian praise of the triune God.

Having observed these examples, we can state the nature of "appropriation" more precisely. Certain works of the Trinity are associated with certain persons of the Trinity because those works specially manifest the personal properties of the specific persons. In the work of creation, a kind of "fathering" of all creatures, the Father's personal property of "paternity" is manifest in a special way. In the work of redemption, a work that involves making "sons" out of slaves, the Son's personal

---

1. Everett Ferguson, *The Rule of Faith: A Guide* (Eugene, OR: Cascade, 2015).

property of "filiation" is manifest in a special way. In the work of sanctification, a work that involves the Father breathing new life into being through his Word, the Spirit's personal property of "spiration" is manifest in a special way. Appropriation, more precisely defined, then, is the special association of certain works of the Trinity with certain persons of the Trinity based on the way certain works specially manifest personal properties of the Trinity (paternity, filiation, and spiration). Thus understood, appropriation not only concerns the works of the triune God. It also concerns the attributes and effects of the triune God.

Missions

Scriptural patterns of appropriating specific works of the triune God to specific persons of the triune God manifest the personal properties of the Trinity in a wonderful way. In turning to scriptural teaching on divine missions, we see another specific application of the Trinitarian shape of God's external works, one that manifests more fully, more wonderfully, the glory and grace of the persons of the Trinity.

"Missions," in the context of Trinitarian theology, refers to "sendings," specifically the Father's sending of the Son to redeem and the Father and Son's sending of the Spirit to sanctify (Gal. 4:4–7). Missions have several features that we must observe if we are to understand them rightly. We may gather the main features of Trinitarian missions by returning to a text discussed in the previous chapter.

John 16:13 describes the mission of the Holy Spirit: "When the Spirit of truth comes, he will guide you into all the truth, for he will not speak from himself, but whatever he hears he will speak, and he will declare to you the things that are to come" (ESV, altered). Note several features of Trinitarian missions indicated by this text. First, as John 16:13 indicates, missions involve the "coming" of a person of the Trinity to us; missions are a mode of a divine person's presence. With respect to the mission of the third person of the Trinity, Jesus promises that the Spirit will come to indwell the disciples (John 14:15–17) and that, by his indwelling presence, he will teach them (John 16:12–15); help, comfort, and advocate for them (John 14:16, 26; 15:26; 16:4–11); and enliven them (John 20:21–23). Second, missions involve a relational reference to creatures. Missions terminate on creatures, in creatures. As we have observed already, the Spirit comes to the disciples in order to indwell them. Third, missions involve a relational reference to God. While missions terminate on creatures, in creatures, missions originate from God, in God. Specifically, missions are extensions in time of a divine person's eternal relation of origin. In the language of John 16:13, the Spirit comes to teach the disciples as one who speaks not "from himself" but rather as one who "hears" from the Father and the Son (John 16:13–15). The Spirit comes to the disciples in time as one who eternally proceeds from the Father and the Son, being sent to the disciples from the Father and the Son (John 14:26; 15:26; 16:7). A mission has an eternal depth (in a divine person's relation of origin) and a temporal shore (in a divine person's coming to dwell among creatures).[2]

In light of this understanding of divine missions, we may summarize the missions of the Son and the Spirit as follows: As the Father eternally begets the Son, so he extends the Son's eternal relation of origin to us by sending him to dwell among us at the fullness of time. God the Father sends God the Son to become incarnate as one of us, to redeem us, and to rule over us as the firstborn Son among many redeemed, adopted siblings. The Son's mission, from his incarnation in the Virgin's womb

---

2. The depth and shore distinction is not original with me, but I cannot locate the original source. This paraphrase may be from an unpublished lecture by John Webster.

to his resurrection and enthronement at the Father's right hand, thus manifests in time his begetting in eternity (Acts 13:30, 33; Rom. 1:4). It is the temporal announcement of the eternal utterance reported in Psalm 2:7.

Moreover, as the Father and the Son eternally breathe forth the Spirit, so they extend the Spirit's eternal relation of origin by sending him to dwell among us in these latter days, thereby crowning the Father's redeeming work in and through the Son to the praise of his glory. God the Father and God the Son send God the Spirit to dwell within us, to pour out into our hearts the Father's love for us in the Son, and to awaken in our hearts a fellowship in the Father's love for the Son and the Son's love for the Father. The Spirit's mission thus manifests in time his double procession in eternity: coming to us from the Father through the Son, the Spirit raises us up in, with, and through the Son to the Father (Gal. 4:6; Eph. 2:18), causing us to crown Jesus Christ as Lord, to the glory of God the Father (1 Cor. 12:3; Phil. 2:11; Rev. 4:10).

To paraphrase Gilles Emery, the divine missions are royal "embassies" in time that convey to us the treasures of God's eternal kingdom.[3] In the missions of the Son and the Spirit, God makes his dwelling among us, bringing the all-sufficiency, glory, and beatitude of his tripersonal life to us, causing us to find our all-sufficiency, glory, and beatitude in him. The missions of the triune God, more than anything else, manifest the grace of God the Father whereby he embraces us as his beloved children, at the cost of his only begotten Son, through the presence of his Holy Spirit, to the glory of his name.

Before concluding our discussion of divine missions, it is important to address a common misunderstanding. Sometimes

3. Gilles Emery, *The Trinitarian Theology of St Thomas Aquinas*, trans. Francesca Aran Murphy (Oxford: Oxford University Press, 2007), 368.

the divine missions are taken as evidence in support of eternal relations of authority and submission. The argument goes something like this: Because the Father sends the Son, and not vice versa, and because the Father and the Son send the Spirit, and not vice versa, the Father has authority over the Son, who submits to the Father, and the Father and the Son have authority over the Spirit, who submits to the Father and the Son. Moreover, because divine missions in time manifest divine relations in eternity, the relations of authority and submission that are manifested in the divine missions in time must also obtain in the relations between the divine persons in eternity.

The problem with this argument is twofold. First of all, this argument fails to understand the nature of divine authority and its status as a common property of all three persons. Divine authority, biblically understood, refers to God's sovereign right to rule over all creatures. Divine authority, thus defined, derives from two sources: from God's being and from God's works. Psalm 95 appeals to both sources in ascribing divine authority to God. According to this psalm, the Lord is "a great King above all gods" (v. 3)—the Lord enjoys the position of supreme cosmic authority—because he is a "great God" (v. 3), because of his majestic being. The Lord also enjoys the position of supreme cosmic authority because of his majestic works.

> In his hand are the depths of the earth;
> > the heights of the mountains are his also.
> The sea is his, for he made it,
> > and his hands formed the dry land. (vv. 4–5)

As God's being and works are common to all three persons of the Trinity, so too is God's authority. As the Father is "Lord of heaven and earth" (Matt. 11:25), so he has granted the Son "all authority in heaven and on earth" (Matt. 28:18; so 11:27).

Indeed, according to the author of Hebrews, "the Holy Spirit" is the selfsame Lord who utters the divine warning published in Psalm 95:7–11:

> Today, if you hear his voice,
>> do not harden your hearts. (Heb. 3:7–8, 15; 4:7; see
>> also Rev. 4:5; 5:6; 22:1–5; with Rev. 2:7, etc.)

Father, Son, and Holy Spirit share one divine sovereignty, one divine authority over all creatures.

The point is further confirmed in John 10:22–30. This passage echoes many of the themes that appear in Psalm 95. The relationship between Jesus and his people is portrayed as a relationship between a shepherd and his "sheep" (John 10:27; see Ps. 95:7) who are in his "hand" (John 10:28–29; see Ps. 95:7). The language of "greatness" is used as well, with Jesus declaring, "My Father . . . is greater than all" (John 10:29; see Ps. 95:3). Finally, John 10 emphasizes that Jesus's sheep will "hear" his "voice" and enter into eternal life (John 10:27–28; see Ps. 95:7, 11). With respect to the present discussion, the important thing to note is that Jesus claims to be "one" with his Father who is "greater than all" (John 10:29–30), a clear echo of Deuteronomy 6:4 ("the LORD is one") that elicits the charge of blasphemy from Jesus's opponents (John 10:31–39). Jesus, the Good Shepherd, is "one" with his Father, who is "greater than all." All that the Father has, Jesus has (John 16:14–15). One Lord with his Father (Deut. 6:4; 1 Cor. 8:6), he is a great God and a great King above all gods (1 Cor. 8:5), the shepherd of his flock, the voice that gives eternal life to all who hear and follow his voice (Ps. 95).

Second of all, the argument that divine missions manifest eternal relations of authority and submission fails to observe the distinction between divine acting and divine mode of acting. In speaking of God's being and attributes, Scripture distinguishes between *what* the divine persons have in common as one God and *how* the divine persons have what they have—that is, the divine persons' distinct modes of having. Thus, for example, according to John 5:26, the Son has the divine attribute of self-existence just as the Father has the divine attribute of self-existence. What distinguishes the Father from the Son is not what they have. What distinguishes the Father from the Son is their distinct personal modes of having what they have. The person of the Father has "life in himself" from himself. The person of the Son has "life in himself" from the Father. What they have, they have in common as one God. Their modes of having are distinguished according to their distinct personal modes of existing.

The same goes for God's actions. Scripture distinguishes between *what* the divine persons do by means of their common agency and *how* the divine persons do what they do—that is, the divine persons' distinct modes of doing. Thus, to consider another example from John 5, Jesus claims, "The Son can do nothing from himself, but only what he sees the Father doing" (John 5:19 ESV, altered). As we saw with respect to the Spirit in John 16:12–15, the Son's not doing anything "from himself" is a reference to his personal mode of acting. As his personal mode of existing is not from himself but from the Father, so his personal mode of acting is not from himself but from the Father. However, far from suggesting that the Son has less authority than the Father, the Son's personal mode of acting from the Father guarantees that he performs all things in common with the Father. As Jesus states in the second half of the verse: "For whatever the Father does, that the Son does likewise" (John 5:19). Whereas the first half of John 5:19 emphasizes the Son's distinct personal mode of operation from the Father's, the second half of John 5:19 emphasizes the Son's common operation with the Father. The point is strengthened in John 5:21, where Jesus states, "As the Father raises the dead and gives them life, so also the Son gives life to whom he will." Here the emphasis is not simply upon the unity of the Father and the Son's works, but upon the Son's authority in performing his works: "The Son gives life to whom he will."

Far then from establishing eternal relations of authority and submission, the divine missions exhibit both the indivisible nature of God's external works and the Trinitarian shape of God's external works.[4] The Son's personal mode of acting from the Father no more undermines the Son's consubstantial authority with the Father than the Son's personal mode of existing from the Father undermines the Son's consubstantial being with the Father. The same goes for the Holy Spirit.[5]

Conclusion

In sum, the divine *missions* are *divine* missions. And this is such a wonderful truth. In the missions of the divine persons, we are not dealing with lesser, subordinate deities to the Father. The

---

4. We must, of course, also speak of the Son's *human* obedience to the Father as a consequence of the incarnation (Phil. 2:6–8), wherein he fulfills his office as the second Adam (Rom. 5:12–21). The Son's human obedience is not unrelated to his temporal divine mission from the Father. Indeed, the former is the goal of the latter. However, the two must be properly distinguished and related if we are to avoid substantial Trinitarian error. For further discussion of these issues, see Michael Allen and Scott R. Swain, "The Obedience of the Eternal Son," *International Journal of Systematic Theology* 15, no. 2 (2013): 114–34; Thomas Joseph White, "The Obedience of the Son," in *The Incarnate Lord: A Thomistic Study in Christology* (Washington, DC: Catholic University of America Press, 2015).

5. There is perhaps a legitimate way of speaking of the persons' "authority" in relation to each other that refers to relations of origin rather than relations of authority and submission. If we speak of one person as "authoring" another person, then we are in safe territory. The Father eternally "authors" the Son in begetting him. The Father and the Son eternally "author" the Spirit in breathing him forth. However, far from establishing different relations of authority and submission, these eternal acts of "authoring" are the means whereby the supreme and single "authority" of God (in the sense I have used it above—i.e., as God's supreme right to rule all creatures) is eternally communicated by the Father to the Son in begetting and by the Father and the Son to the Spirit in breathing. For further discussion of these matters within the context of Thomas Aquinas's theology, see John Baptist Ku, *God the Father in the Theology of St. Thomas Aquinas* (New York: Peter Lang, 2013).

one who came to die for us on the cross is the Lord of glory, consubstantial with the Father (1 Cor. 2:8). The Good Shepherd who gave his life for the sheep is a great God and a great King above all gods (John 10:11). "One of the Trinity suffered for us," the old saying goes. Likewise, the one who came to dwell within us is the Lord and giver of life, consubstantial with the Father and the Son, present to reveal divine glory, to pour out divine love, to bring us into the very Holy of Holies of communion with the Father and the Son through communion with himself (John 6:63; 16:12–15; Rom. 5:5; 2 Cor. 13:14). This is eternal life, to know the Father by the indwelling Spirit through Jesus Christ whom he sent (John 17:3).

8

The End of God's Triune Work

Christians praise the triune God because he is their supreme good (Ps. 16:1–2), worthy of all praise, and their supreme end, that to which both they and all things are directed by God's supreme providence in nature, grace, and glory: "From him and through him and to him are all things. To him be glory forever" (Rom. 11:36).

In the previous chapter, we considered the triune shape of God's work. Here we will consider the triune end of God's work. To address this topic, I will discuss, first, the ultimate end of God's triune work, God himself; second, the ultimate beneficiaries of God's triune work, God's beloved children; and, third, the means whereby the triune God communicates the benefits of his work to his beloved children, the ministry of word and sacrament, received by faith, hope, and love.

The Ultimate End of God's Triune Work

God is a builder. The first building project Scripture portrays is God's work of creation in Genesis 1–2. Reflecting on the construction imagery in Scripture's opening chapters, Psalm 104 extends the imagery, describing God in the work of creation as "stretching out the heavens like a tent" (v. 2), laying "the beams of his chambers on the waters" (v. 3), and setting "the earth on its foundations" (v. 5). What kind of building project is creation? Again, Genesis 1–2 offers suggestive answers that later scriptures amplify and clarify. In constructing the heavens and earth, God the great King constructs a palace. The Lord declares in Isaiah:

> Heaven is my throne,
>   and the earth is my footstool. . . .
> All these things my hand has made. (Isa. 66:1–2)

Moreover, because this palace is the palace of God, creation is also a temple, the place where God's glory dwells, the place where his priestly image bearers serve him (Gen. 2:4–25).[1] This sacred design becomes especially clear when we look at the final building project Scripture portrays, the making of the new heaven and earth, which Revelation 21–22 portrays as a cosmic Holy of Holies, the palace-temple of the triune King, where God's redeemed children see his face and serve him as a kingdom of priests in a state of endless Sabbath delight (Rev. 22:1–5).[2]

Homes are built for a reason, and this is true of God's eschatological building project as well. God the Father has given a bride to God the Son, and God's cosmic palace-temple is constructed to be their marital habitation (Rev. 19:6–10; 21:2). Within the divine King's cosmic palace-temple, those united in

---

1. L. Michael Morales, *The Tabernacle Pre-Figured: Cosmic Mountain Ideology in Genesis and Exodus* (Leuven: Peeters, 2012).

2. G. K. Beale, "Theological Conclusions: The Physical Temple as a Foreshadowing of God's and Christ's Presence as the True Temple," in *The Temple and the Church's Mission*, New Studies in Biblical Theology (Downers Grove, IL: InterVarsity Press, 2004).

marriage to Jesus Christ are welcomed into God's household as Jesus's redeemed siblings (Song 4:9), God the Father's own beloved sons and daughters (Rom. 8:29; 2 Cor. 6:16–18). Already God's beloved children have received the highest proof of the Father's love for them in the sacrifice of his beloved Son (Rom. 8:32), and already they have received the seal of their eternal inheritance in the Holy Spirit (Eph. 1:13–14). Consequently, they purify themselves like a bride who longs for the day when the bridegroom will appear to receive them into his Father's house, where they will drink in his Spirit and rejoice in his eternal love (Eph. 5:27; Titus 2:13; 1 John 3:1–3; Rev. 22:1–5):

> Let him kiss me with the kisses of his mouth!
> For your love is better than wine;
>> your anointing oils are fragrant;
> your name is oil poured out;
>> therefore virgins love you.
> Draw me after you; let us run.
>> The king has brought me into his chambers.
>> (Song 1:2–4)

Homes are built for a reason. And this home is built for union and communion between the triune God and his beloved, redeemed children, for the marital bliss of Christ and his bride.

The union and communion between the triune God and his beloved children, the marital bliss of Christ and his bride—these are indeed ends of God's great building project, of God's external works; and creation itself longs to see this end realized (Rom. 8:18–22). However, neither the union and communion between God and his children nor the marital joy of Christ and his bride is the ultimate, final end of God's external works. The triune God himself, and the triune God alone, is the ultimate and final end of his sacred house-building project, of the marriage of Christ and his bride, and of the union and communion between the triune God and his people.

"From him and through him and *to him* are all things" (Rom. 11:36). God is the great builder in this building project: "From him . . . are all things." And God engages in this work in his own strength, not in the strength of another: "Through him . . . are all things." God's own wisdom provides the sole blueprint for this building project: "the depth of the riches and wisdom and knowledge of God" (Rom. 11:33). And God's own will—his "unsearchable . . . judgments"—determine the ends and means for fulfilling this building project. Though many subordinate ends are pursued, and though many works are accomplished in bringing this building project to pass, the construction of God's cosmic palace-temple is ultimately and finally aimed at one end: God himself, the alpha and the omega, the first and the last, the beginning and the end (Rev. 22:13). "To him be glory forever" (Rom. 11:36).

And it could not be any other way. All agents act in view of an end. And, in any course of action, the final end is the one judged by the agent to be the supreme good, the supreme reason for pursuing that particular course of action. Because God alone is the supreme good, he must be the supreme end of all his external works in creation, redemption, and consummation.

Because God himself is the supreme good, nothing outside God himself could be the ultimate end of his external works. The doctrine of the Trinity does not challenge this proposition but only confirms it. The doctrine of the Trinity does, however, illumine our understanding of God's ultimate end, not by illumining something outside God himself but by illumining something inside God himself, namely, the three persons of the Trinity and their eternal, mutual life of knowledge and love.

According to Holy Scripture, God's external works in creation, redemption, and consummation not only have a triune shape; they also have a triune end.

Romans 8:28–30 describes the "good" toward which God works "all things." In accordance with God's sovereign foreknowledge and predestination, the good toward which God directs all things includes the calling, justification, and glorification of God's elect. It also includes their conformity to the image of his Son, an effect produced by God through sanctification and glorification. However, the final good in the ordered series of goods governed by God's saving providence is Trinitarian in nature. The supreme good the Father perceives, the final end to which he directs our calling, justification, sanctification, and glorification, is "his Son" and his Son's sovereign installation and manifestation as "the firstborn among many brothers" (Rom. 8:29). We often think of the Son's incarnate, redeeming, and ruling works, as well as the multitude of spiritual benefits procured for us thereby, as being ordered to our salvation. And they are, to a certain degree: Jesus became incarnate, died, and rose again to save us. But our salvation is not the final ordering principle of the works Jesus performs or the benefits he procures. Our salvation is finally ordered to Jesus, God's beloved Son, the supreme good eternally loved by the Father in the Spirit, the final end appointed by the Father in the Spirit in his eternal decree, the final end toward which the Father in the Spirit moves all things in his providence. All of God's external works and the new creation itself are a theater for his glory, "that in everything he might be preeminent" (Col. 1:18), "to the glory of God the Father" (Phil. 2:11).

God—who, in eternity, crowns his beloved Son in the Spirit—creates, redeems, and consummates the world in order that he might, in time, crown his beloved Son in the Spirit, installing him as "the highest of the kings of the earth" (Ps. 89:27), the heir of the nations (Ps. 2:8), the head of the body (Eph. 1:22–23), and the husband of the bride (Eph. 5:32): "the most handsome of the sons of men" (Ps. 45:2), the loveliest, most desirable, most satisfying object of all loves, desires, or satisfactions. There is no greater good, there is no higher end. And so God's beloved Son, who knows how to pray that the Father's crowning purpose will be accomplished, prays for his elect siblings in John 17:24–26 that they might see the glory given him by the Father in love before the foundation of the world, that they might share the Father's love for the Son, and that the Son might dwell within them. Because the Father loves the Son in the Spirit, he loves us (John 3:16). And the Father loves us that we too might share his love for the Son in the Spirit. In this the Father is glorified; in this the fruit of the Spirit is exhibited; in this our joy is made full (John 15:8, 11).

The Ultimate Beneficiaries of God's Triune Work

God, the triune God—the Father who crowns his beloved Son in the Spirit—is the final end of God's external works. The next question we must ask is, who benefits?

The questions of ends and beneficiaries are distinguishable. A builder might construct a house for different ends and different beneficiaries. He might build a house so that he can live in it. In this case, the builder is both end and beneficiary. A builder might also build a house in order to sell it so that someone else might live in it. In this case, the purchaser (who occupies the house) is end and beneficiary, while the builder also benefits (he makes money by selling the house). To cite but one further example, a builder might build a house in order to give it to someone who has no home and who has no means of purchasing a home. In this case, the recipient of the home is both end and beneficiary, whereas the builder is neither. His work is an act of charity.

God is the supreme end of his house-building project. Temples are made for gods, and this temple is made for God. Is he also the supreme beneficiary? Is he perhaps a minor beneficiary? The answer to both questions is no. The triune God cannot be the beneficiary of his external works for the same reason that he must be the ultimate end of his external works: his supreme sufficiency, glory, and beatitude. In and of himself, in the perfect fellowship of the Father, the Son, and the Holy Spirit, God enjoys all sufficiency, all glory, all beatitude. He could not possibly benefit from his external works, because he is supreme benefit without them. As Paul asks in Romans 11:35,

> Who has given a gift to him
> that he might be repaid?

The answer is *no one*. Nothing enriches God; nothing adds to his glory; nothing increases his happiness (Job 22:2; 35:6–7; 41:11). God is not "served by human hands, as though he needed anything" (Acts 17:25). God plus the world is not more sufficient, more glorious, or more blessed than God minus the world.[3] Therefore, God's external works, in their endless variety and also in their cosmic totality, are a supreme act of charity, an act of the most liberal generosity.[4]

Who, then, benefits? The answer of course must be God's beloved children. The heart of the blessed Trinity is to benefit us by giving himself to us. This is the love of the Father. This is the grace of our Lord Jesus Christ. This is the fellowship of the

---

3. Robert Sokolowski, *The God of Faith and Reason: Foundations of Christian Theology* (Washington, DC: Catholic University of America Press, 1995), 8–9.

4. Thomas Aquinas, *Summa Theologica*, trans. Fathers of the English Dominican Province (New York: Benzinger, 1948), I, q. 44, art. 4, ad 1.

Holy Spirit (2 Cor. 13:14). The glory that the Father manifests in predestination, that the Son manifests in redemption, and that the Spirit manifests in sanctification is the glory of God's free, boundless, generous grace (Eph. 1:3–14). In eternity, God the Father crowns God the Son by God the Holy Spirit and, in so doing, is eternally blessed. In time, God the Father crowns God the Son by God the Holy Spirit, manifesting and communicating his eternal blessedness and, in so doing, making us eternally blessed in him. In the end, God's supreme end in God's external works and our supreme good do not stand in a competitive, contrastive relation because they are one. How blessed are the people whose God is the Lord (Ps. 144:15)!

How the Triune God Communicates His Triune Benefits to Us

If the triune God is the supreme end of his external works, and if his beloved children are the supreme beneficiaries of his external works, then how does the triune God communicate his triune benefits to us? How may we obtain God's triune benefits? The answer is that God himself must do it. Divine goods (the persons of the Trinity and their various gifts) can be communicated to us only by divine agency. And this is what God does. All the goods that God seeks to give us God himself proclaims in his word and bestows by his Spirit (James 1:17–18). More specifically, the action of communicating divine goods to God's people, though indivisible in nature, is appropriated to the Holy Spirit. The saving blessings purposed by the Father and purchased by the Son are communicated to us by the presence of the Spirit (2 Cor. 13:14; Eph. 1:3–14). The Holy Spirit consummates God's triune work of salvation by communicating to God's children all that the Father has accomplished for them in the Son, all that the Father offers to them in the Son.

Though God himself, in the person of the Holy Spirit, must communicate God's gifts to us, God is pleased to use creaturely instruments as means whereby the divine agency communicates divine goods to us.

In chapter 6, we observed that a Trinitarian spirituality is a spirituality that follows the Word because it knows that the Holy Spirit proceeds from the Word and that the Holy Spirit seeks to glorify the Word. For this reason, a Trinitarian spirituality is also one that attends to the means appointed by God in his word to communicate every spiritual blessing to his people.

The Holy Spirit communicates the blessings of God to the children of God through both "exhibitive instruments" and "receptive instruments." Exhibitive instruments, also called "means of grace," are creaturely means whereby God the Father presents and offers God the Son to us. Receptive instruments are creaturely means whereby we welcome and receive God the Father as he presents God the Son to us. Both exhibitive instruments and receptive instruments are effectual to the communication of God's gifts to his people by the presence and power of his Spirit, which is why prayer for the Spirit's help is essential to the effective employment of divinely appointed instruments.

Exhibitive instruments include the preaching of the word and the ministry of the sacraments. Preaching announces all that the Father has accomplished in the Son and summons hearers to receive all that the Father promises them in the Son (Luke 24:46–47; Rom. 1:1–6; 1 Cor. 15:1–4). The object of preaching is the announcement of something accomplished outside us, there and then, in the incarnation, death, resurrection, and exaltation of Jesus Christ, God's eternal Son. This announcement includes the promise of life in his name (John 20:31; 1 John 5:11–12).[5]

---

5. Walter Brueggemann, *Israel's Praise: Doxology against Idolatry and Ideology* (Philadelphia: Fortress, 1988), 32.

Preaching ultimately has an eminently personal object, the Son of God himself (Rom. 1:3). It is not simply "Christ crucified" that Paul "placards" in the preaching of the gospel but "Jesus Christ and him crucified" (1 Cor. 2:2; see also Gal. 3:1). Preaching is God the Father proclaiming God the Son in the power of God the Spirit through sent human messengers.[6] Preaching is "God making his appeal through us"—those who are appointed to serve as "ambassadors for Christ" (2 Cor. 5:20).

Though the object of preaching is God's beloved Son and the announcement of something accomplished in him outside us there and then, the end of preaching is to effect a transformation inside us here and now.[7] In the power of the Holy Spirit, the proclamation of the word brings about its own reception, causing us to receive Jesus Christ by faith, and with him all the blessings of the gospel, and causing us to turn "to God from idols to serve the living and true God, and to wait for his Son from heaven . . . , Jesus who delivers us from the wrath to come" (1 Thess. 1:9–10; see also Rom. 1:5; 10:17). Preaching ultimately has an eminently personal end: to summon the bride to embrace her beloved bridegroom and, in embracing him, to receive a divine bounty in union and communion with him (Ps. 45).

The sacraments of baptism and the Lord's Supper signify and seal the same blessings presented to us in Scripture, applying those blessings personally to members of the covenant community. Baptism signifies and seals to us all the blessings purchased for us by Jesus Christ in the gospel: justification, adoption, sanctification, and glorification (1 Cor. 6:11; Gal. 3:26–29; Titus 3:4–7). Ultimately baptism signifies and seals to us an eminently personal end: union and communion with the

---

6. Adapted from J. I. Packer, *God Has Spoken: Revelation and the Bible*, 3rd ed. (Grand Rapids, MI: Baker, 1998), 91.

7. Brueggemann, *Israel's Praise*, 32.

three persons of the Trinity—we are baptized "into" the name of the triune God (Matt. 28:19 ESV margin note). The Lord's Supper is a memorial rite whereby God the incarnate and exalted Son comes to us and blesses us by God the Spirit (see Ex. 20:24; Luke 22:19; 24:30). The Lord's Supper is a sacrament of spiritual nourishment, the means whereby we receive spiritual food and drink through the ordinary elements of bread and wine (1 Cor. 10:1–4). By the mouth of faith, we partake of and commune in the body and blood of the incarnate Son himself as he is presented to us by the Father in the gospel (1 Cor. 10:16). The Supper thus has an eminently personal end as well, insofar as it is the sacrament of Communion with the Lord who meets us at his table (Ps. 23:4–5).

The Spirit who makes word and sacrament effectual in communicating all that the Father gives us in the Son also enables us to receive all that the Father gives us in the Son. Faith alone receives, rests in, and relies upon Jesus Christ as he is offered to us in the gospel, as well as all the benefits that God offers us in him (John 1:11–13; Eph. 2:8–9). Faith is the principal receptive instrument whereby those who seek the triune God receive the triune God, the exceedingly great reward that is offered to us in the gospel (Gen. 15:1; Heb. 11:6). The faith that alone receives God and the good things offered to us by God in the gospel does not remain alone but is a principle from which other virtues spring forth. Faith begets "a living hope" (1 Pet. 1:3; see also 1:23–25), which waits with eager anticipation for "the appearing of the glory of our great God and Savior Jesus Christ" (Titus 2:13).

> O my Strength, I will watch for you,
>> for you, O God, are my fortress.
> My God in his steadfast love will meet me. (Ps. 59:9–10)

Faith also gives rise to love: "The aim of our charge is love that issues from a pure heart and a good conscience and a sincere faith" (1 Tim. 1:5). Love rejoices and relishes in the God who loves us and gives himself to us in the gospel. Love also welcomes those whom God, in giving us himself, gives to us in order that, with them, we might share all the goods of our common life in him (Mark 12:28–34; Rom. 12:9–10; 15:7; 1 John 4:10–12). As faith receives the Lord, so love learns to walk in the Lord (Col. 2:6–7), measuring the immeasurable boundaries of his goodness (Pss. 16:5–6; 36:5–6), taking note of the unshakeable security that is ours in him (Pss. 16:1–2; 36:7), drinking deeply from the river of his infinite delights (Pss. 16:11; 36:8–9).

The blessings that the triune God communicates to us now by grace through faith, by means of the ministry of word and sacrament, he will one day communicate to us in glory through sight, apart from creaturely instruments, by the glory of his own manifest presence (Ps. 84; 1 Cor. 13:8–13; Titus 2:13; Rev. 21:22–22:5). In that sacred palace-temple constructed by the triune God, the love of God the Father, the grace of our Lord Jesus Christ, and the fellowship of the Holy Spirit will be "with" us all forever and will endure forever (1 Cor. 13:8; 2 Cor. 13:14). Love is the crown jewel bestowed by the Father on the Son in the Spirit. And love is the crown jewel of our life with the Father in the Son by the Spirit (John 17:24–26). "So now faith, hope, and love abide, these three; but the greatest of these is love" (1 Cor. 13:13).

Conclusion

The triune God alone is the ultimate end of all his works, the supreme benefit he gives, the supreme benefit that can be received. God the Father manifests his glory in God the Son and,

through him, communicates his blessings in God the Spirit because the triune God alone is supremely worthy of showing,
and supremely worthy of sharing with others. As this one thing,
God the blessed Trinity, is the final end of all God's ways and
all God's purposes, it should be the "one thing" we seek as well,

> that I may dwell in the house of the LORD
>   all the days of my life,
> to gaze upon the beauty of the LORD
>   and to inquire in his temple. (Ps. 27:4)

> You have said, "Seek my face."
> My heart says to you,
>   "Your face, LORD, do I seek." (Ps. 27:8)

Glossary

active spiration. Though not a *personal property* (q.v.) in the strict sense of the term, because it is held in common by the *person* (q.v.) of the Father and the *person* of the Son, *active spiration* identifies the Father and the Son as the *persons* who eternally breathe out the *person* of the Holy Spirit.

filiation. The *personal property* (q.v.) of the Son that identifies him as the divine *person* (q.v.) eternally begotten by the *person* of the Father. *Filiation* names the Son's distinctive personal *relation of origin* (q.v.).

mission. In Trinitarian theology, this term refers to one divine *person* (q.v.) "sending" another divine *person* in time to accomplish God's undivided work of salvation: the Father sends the Son to become our incarnate Redeemer and Lord; the Father and the Son send the Spirit to indwell, enliven, and sanctify us. In the *missions* of the Trinity, the eternal *relations of origin* (q.v.) are extended to creatures in time: the Father who eternally begets the Son sends his Son to us in order that we might receive the gift of adoption; the Father and the Son who eternally breathe out the Holy Spirit send the Holy Spirit to us in order that we might be sanctified for fellowship with the triune God.

passive spiration. The *personal property* (q.v.) of the Holy Spirit that identifies him as the divine *person* (q.v.) eternally breathed out by the *person* of the Father and the *person* of the Son. *Passive spiration* names the Spirit's distinctive personal *relation of origin* (q.v.).

paternity. The *personal property* (q.v.) of the Father that identifies him as the divine *person* (q.v.) who eternally begets the *person* of the Son. While the Father eternally begets the Son (and, with the Son, eternally breathes out the Spirit), the Father himself has no *relation of origin* (q.v.).

person. In Trinitarian theology, this term identifies that which distinguishes the Father, the Son, and the Spirit from each other. Though the term has various secular uses in the ancient and modern worlds, its use in Trinitarian theology likely originates in the practice of *prosopological exegesis* (q.v.). According to Boethius's influential definition, a person is "an individual substance of a rational nature." In other words, a *person* is not merely an individual *something*; a *person* is a certain kind of individual, an individual *someone* characterized by and worthy of knowledge and love. Because that which individuates the persons of the Trinity is each person's *relation of origin* (q.v.), Thomas Aquinas defines a Trinitarian person as a "subsisting relation."

personal property. The unique identifying feature of each *person* (q.v.) of the Trinity that distinguishes him from the other two. The Father's *personal property* is *paternity* (q.v.); the Son's *personal property* is *filiation* (q.v.); the Spirit's *personal property* is *passive spiration* (q.v.).

prosopological exegesis. An ancient reading strategy commonly employed by Greco-Roman readers, New Testament authors, and the church fathers, this strategy involves clarifying the otherwise ambiguous identity of speech agents in conversations recorded in a sacred text. *Prosopological exegesis* addresses questions such as Who is speaking in this text? and To whom is the speaker speaking in this text?

relation(s) of origin. That (and that alone) which distinguishes one *person* (q.v.) of the Trinity from other *persons* of the Trinity is the manner in which he is eternally related to another *person* of the Trinity as his personal principle or source. The Father has no eternal personal principle or source. The Father is the eternal personal principle or source of the Son through begetting the Son. The Father and the Son are the eternal personal principle or source of the Holy Spirit through breathing the Holy Spirit.

Further Reading

Augustine, *The Trinity*. Translated by Edmund Hill. Brooklyn, NY: New City, 1991. In what is the most influential book on the Trinity in the West, Augustine elaborates and defends the scriptural foundations of "pro-Nicene" Trinitarian theology and examines whether and how reason can more fully understand what faith receives on the basis of Holy Scripture. (Intermediate/advanced)

Beckwith, Carl L. *The Holy Trinity*. Ft. Wayne, IN: The Luther Academy, 2016. The best contemporary survey of the biblical, historical, and dogmatic dimensions of the doctrine of the Trinity. (Introductory)

Emery, Gilles, *The Trinitarian Theology of St Thomas Aquinas*. Translated by Francesca Aran Murphy. Oxford: Oxford University Press, 2007. Exposition and analysis of the Trinitarian thought of one of the church's most significant theologians by a leading Dominican scholar. (Advanced)

Emery, Gilles, and Matthew Levering, eds. *The Oxford Handbook of the Trinity*. Oxford: Oxford University Press, 2011. Up-to-date overviews of biblical, historical, dogmatic, and practical dimensions of Trinitarian theology. Especially important for the student of Trinitarian theology is J. Warren Smith's contribution, "The Trinity in the Fourth-Century Fathers." (Intermediate)

Gregory of Nazianzus, *On God and Christ: The Five Theological Orations and Two Letters to Cledonius*. Crestwood, NY: St Vladimir's Seminary Press, 2002. Five sermons on the Trinity delivered on the eve of the Council of Constantinople. (Introductory/intermediate)

Sanders, Fred, *The Triune God*. New Studies in Dogmatics. Grand Rapids, MI: Zondervan Academic, 2016. Today's leading theologian of the Trinity applies the biblical-theological concept of "mystery" to a modern theological problem (i.e., the relationship between the immanent and economic Trinity). The result is an architectonic framework for understanding the unfolding revelation of the Trinity in relation to the Old and New Testaments. (Intermediate)

Trueman, Carl, and Brandon Crowe, *The Essential Trinity: New Testament Foundations and Practical Relevance*. Phillipsburg, NJ: P&R, 2017. A survey of New Testament teaching on the Trinity that includes several synthetic and practical chapters as well. (Introductory)

General Index

Scripture Index

Short Studies in Systematic Theology

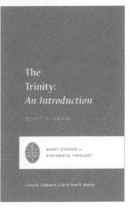

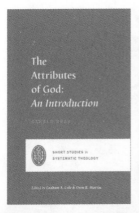

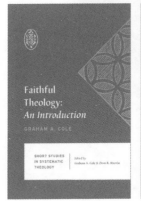

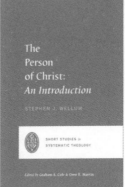

For more information, visit **crossway.org**.